Hereford Locomotive Shed

HEREFORD LOCOMOTIVE SHED

ENGINES AND TRAIN WORKINGS

Steve Bartlett

PEN & SWORD
TRANSPORT

Dedication

To Hereford's shed staff and footplate crews, who worked in difficult and challenging circumstances against a background of a much-changing industry.

First published in Great Britain in 2017 by
Pen & Sword Transport
An imprint of Pen & Sword Books Ltd
47 Church Street
Barnsley
South Yorkshire
S70 2AS

ISBN 978 1 47387 5 555

Printed and bound by Replika Press Pvt. Ltd

Typeset in Palatino

Pen & Sword Books Ltd incorporates the imprints of Pen & Sword Archaeology, Atlas, Aviation, Battleground, Discovery, Family History, History, Maritime, Military, Naval, Politics, Railways, Select, Social History, Transport, True Crime, and Claymore Press, Frontline Books, Leo Cooper, Praetorian Press, Remember When, Seaforth Publishing and Wharncliffe.

For a complete list of Pen and Sword titles please contact:
Pen and Sword Books Limited
47 Church Street, Barnsley, South Yorkshire S70 2AS, England
E-mail: enquiries@pen-and-sword.co.uk
Website: www.pen-and-sword.co.uk

Contents

Acknowledgments

This story has been built around personal memories of the Hereford railway scene, and of Hereford Shed in particular between 1958 and the 1964 shed closure. These have been strengthened, indeed in some cases, old mysteries solved, by, over fifty years later, delving into official industry records, supported by invaluable assistance from like-minded individuals.

Regrettably, I was a poor photographer myself, but have managed to gather over 200 photographs from many sources to bring the Hereford railway scene to life. My grateful thanks go to those who gave me access to their private collections, as well as assistance from several photographic libraries. John Goss was particularly helpful, with his previously mostly unpublished Hereford photographs being around a third of those used. He was a contemporary Herefordian using a much better camera and photographic skills than I, and it is no wonder that he became a professional photographer. I am also grateful to well-known railway photographer Ben Ashworth, who let me use some of his memorable Herefordshire branch line images. Thanks for photographic contributions also go to: Terry Walsh for the R.G. Nelson collection; Laurence Waters from the Great Western Trust; Paul Shackcloth from the Manchester Locomotive Society; David Postle from Kidderminster Railway Museum; and David Cross for the images taken by his father, Derek Cross. Further contributions have come from Michael Jennings, Ron Herbert, R.H.G. Simpson, John Hodge and Roy Palmer; apologies if anyone has been omitted. Richard Soddy is thanked for the drawing of shed plans and maps. I must also mention Rex and Andrew Kennedy of *Steam Days* magazine, who have published my articles for the last ten years and gave me the confidence to tackle a full length volume. Thanks also to my wife Lin who always supported me despite losing me for weeks on end immersed in the Hereford railway scene.

Finally, thanks to retired Hereford footplate men who generously shared their memories with me – for it is also their story that is told here.

HEREFORD RAIL ROUTES

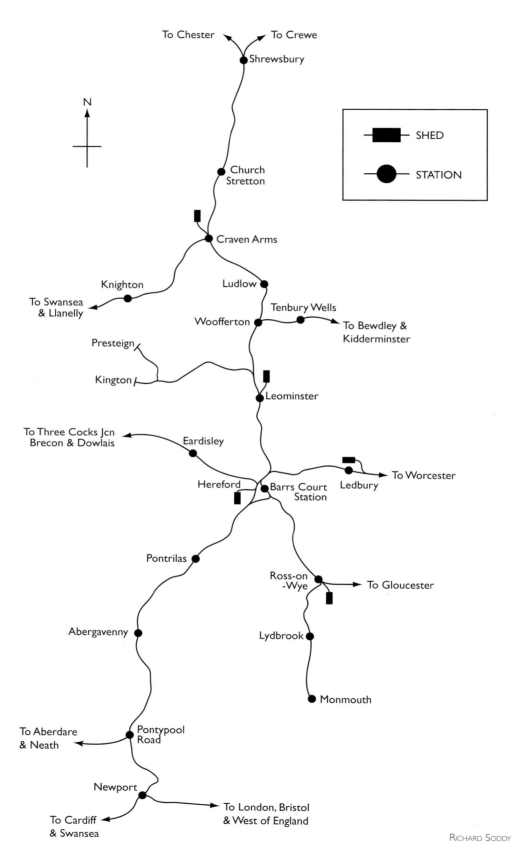

Richard Soddy

Introduction and Shed Layout

I spent most of my early years in South Wales with railways most definitely in my blood. I can remember on Saturday mornings at around ten years of age going with my father to the unassuming single-storey building that was the Neath Running and Maintenance District Office. The 87 District stretched from Neath through Swansea and covered all West Wales depots. My father, an ex-GWR Swindon Works apprentice, was the Assistant District Running and Maintenance Officer. It was 1958 and the journey to the

Hereford Shed viewed from the north on 29 January 1961, with the Hereford avoiding line in the foreground looking towards Red Hill Junction and South Wales. The main shed building is in the background behind the signal box, with the impressive coaling stage on the right and the outline of Bulmer's Cider Factory behind. Meanwhile, on the left, a local 2F 1600 0-6-0PT makes a head shunt out of Barton Down Sidings. M. Hale/Great Western Trust

office would see me precariously perched on the back of his rather ancient black upright pre-war bicycle. One particular Saturday morning, I recall a commotion mid-morning and being hurried down to the small Neath N&B sub-shed located beyond the office. There, sitting squarely on the ballast, where it had split a pair of points coming onto shed, was one of Brecon's 2MT 465XX 2-6-0s. It had arrived at around 9.40am with the 8.5am (SO) Brecon-Neath Riverside service and was shortly booked to work the 11.25am (SO) return train. The quietly-simmering offender was surrounded by a huddle of railwaymen deep in conversation scratching their heads as to what to do next. I just excitedly took the scene in for what it was worth and would not have thought about how a replacement engine could be found at such short notice.

Roll forward twenty years to the depths of winter in the late 1970s. Then, as a youthful Area Operations Manager, I found myself with a Swansea Eastern Depot crew on an English Electric Type 3 Class 37 diesel in that same area on the edge of the Brecon Beacons. We were surrounded by deep snow and had brought the Landore breakdown vans to this remote location to rescue another English Electric Type 3 diesel that had become derailed in a snowdrift. Ahead of me, the breakdown gang were hand-shovelling snow away to find a stable base on which to position the jacks for lifting and re-railing the offending engine. The whole job was professionally completed in a couple of hours before returning to the depot.

You may wonder what the relevance of all this has to the story of Hereford Shed. Well, from the age of eleven in 1959 through to Hereford's shed closure in 1964, I would study intently from behind shed boundary railings and, later, venture around the Shed itself at least several times a week. From these

visits, memories were stored and copious records were kept that have survived to this day. These memories alone might have resulted in a somewhat rose-tinted recollection. However, a lifetime of later working in railway operations, and timetable and resource planning, albeit in the diesel era, has enabled me to put a more reasoned and in-depth interpretation of those rail operations of long ago.

I was by this time boarding at Hereford Cathedral School to provide a more settled base for my education as my railway family moved from Neath to Gloucester and later on to Bristol. On all those Hereford Shed visits, I never once revealed my family link although, contrary to common practice, I would always seek permission to go around the Shed. Standing as tall as possible behind the booking-on office counter, I would wait nervously, glancing around at drivers reading late notice cases or roster sheets listing their diagrammed workings. Eagerly consulted by them would be the daily alterations sheet that could move their booking-on time by several hours each way and place them on a different job to the weekly roster. Most important was the special notice case, listing late temporary speed-restriction information. The foreman, in his long dust jacket, might be on the phone or talking to the depot clerk, and you kept your fingers crossed he was in a good mood. If it was Les Parry or a youngish driver that regularly covered the foreman's job, then you knew you were alright. Little did I know that the paths of Les Parry and I would cross years later when I became a railwayman myself and he a Shift Movements Supervisor at the station.

The depot was located remotely from the passenger station on what was known as the Hereford avoiding line. This was a freight-only route, signalled under the

HEREFORD AREA

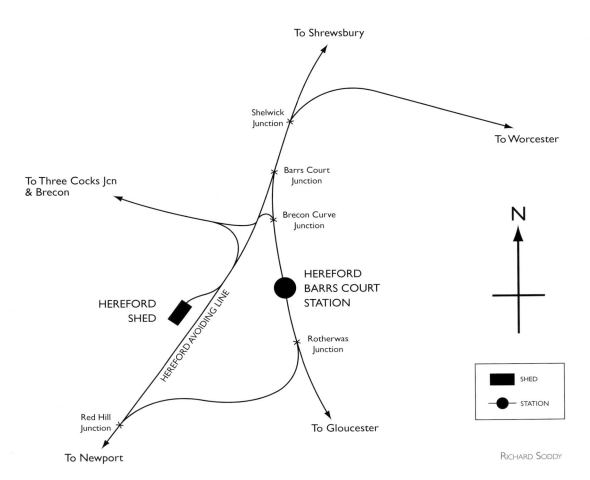

To Shrewsbury

To Worcester

Shelwick
Junction

Barrs Court
Junction

Brecon Curve
Junction

To Three Cocks Jcn
& Brecon

N

HEREFORD
BARRS COURT
STATION

HEREFORD
SHED

HEREFORD AVOIDING LINE

Rotherwas
Junction

| | SHED |
| | STATION |

Red Hill
Junction

To Newport

To Gloucester

RICHARD SODDY

permissive block arrangements. It left the main line at Red Hill Junction on the approaches from South Wales and rejoined it at Barrs Court Junction north of the passenger station. From Red Hill Junction, the avoiding line crossed the Wye by the Hunderton river bridge, from where it ran on a high embankment and under Barton Road Bridge. On the far side of this on the left-hand side was the locomotive depot, with Barton Sidings to the right where a shunting pilot busied itself. Long-distance freight trains would come to a stand near the shed exit by the signal box to take water and train crew relief. Being a permissively-signalled line, a second and even a third freight train

could be allowed to proceed from Red Hill Junction under caution, instructed to be prepared to stop short of any train ahead in the section. This could, at busy times, result in a queue of two or three freight trains, nose to tail, stretching from the Shed back to the Hunderton river bridge.

Our school sports field was located below the railway embankment and on many occasions I was faced with the dilemma of whether to disappear into a rugby loose scrum or identify a rare engine on a passing freight train. One incident firmly embedded in my memory is seeing, high up on that embankment, the front end of an ex-GWR 5MT

4-6-0 buried deep into what remained of a decimated brake van at the rear of a stationary freight train ahead. Clearly the 'proceed with caution' instruction hadn't worked too well on this occasion. It was only whilst researching this book that I discovered that the incident had occurred in October 1959, in the hours of darkness in river-bound fog and poor visibility. The offending engine was Pontypool Road's No. 6872 *Crawley Grange*. The Pontypool Road footplate crew had been shocked, but fortunately unhurt. Even more luckily, the guard from the train in front had already left his van to walk forward to find his relief.

The Hereford avoiding line looking towards Hunderton River Bridge and Red Hill Junction in 1961. The photograph is taken from Barton Road Bridge, with the Shed situated behind the photographer on the up side. Hereford High School's sports field is to the left and Hereford Cathedral School's field just out of view on the right. Meanwhile Oxley's 4MT 2-6-0 No. 7339 approaches with a freight train from South Wales to the West Midlands, which will shortly be stopping for water and probably train crew relief. JOHN GOSS

Before proceeding to the Shed itself, we'll pause and set the Hereford railway scene in context. Hereford was an important intermediate calling point for both long-distance passenger and freight trains on the North & West route from South Wales to Shrewsbury and Crewe. There were both day and overnight express passenger services from the West of England to Manchester and Liverpool via the Severn Tunnel, and also from South Wales to Manchester and Liverpool, coming up the same route from Newport. As far as Hereford there were also passenger services from South Wales to Birmingham Snow Hill and long-distance freight trains to the West Midlands. These left the main route at Shelwick Junction, north of Hereford, heading for Worcester. A two-hourly express passenger service started at Hereford for Paddington, also routed via Shelwick Junction and Worcester. The majority of freight trains from South Wales took the previously-described freight-only Hereford avoiding line, although some ran via Barrs Court and the passenger station. The Brecon Curve, which linked the station with the Hereford avoiding line gave direct access to the shed for light engine movements, inter-yard freight trips and the Brecon branch service. A second and more significant branch line left the station for Gloucester via Rotherwas Junction. The map of the area sets this into context, and shows the position of the depot's various sub-sheds and the branch lines they served.

The British Locomotive Shed Directory from Ian Allan Publishing was the railway enthusiast's bible for finding your way to a particular shed as this extract shows:

'The shed is on the west side of the Hereford avoiding line (goods) by Barton Goods Yard. Turn left outside the station along Station Road and right into Commercial Road. Continue along High Town and High Street into Eign Street. Turn left into Victoria Road, right into Barton Street and continue into Barton Road. The shed entrance is a gate (actually a steeply-graded roadway) on the right-hand side just past the railway under-bridge. Walking time 25 minutes.'

Depots were not always located close to main stations and could involve lengthy walks or local bus journeys, particularly when located on freight-only lines as was the case at Hereford. It was quite a long trek from the station here and the quoted twenty-five minutes was rather optimistic. The fact no passenger trains passed the site, combined with this remoteness from the station, made Hereford a less commonly visited shed for many enthusiasts.

Now would be an appropriate time for us to take the steep access road down to the shed from Barton Road. Immediately on the left was the train crew booking-on point, where the shift shed running foreman was to be found, followed by doors to the driver and firemen's mess room, and next for cleaners and shed ancillary staff. On the first floor was the Shed Master's personal office and somewhere I never actually found the clerical support staff. This building had once been the main office of the Newport, Abergavenny and Hereford Railway, later absorbed by the GWR. We will return to the Repair Shop, which came next on the left, later and head with youthful enthusiasm for the dark depths of the main shed building. This was an eight road stone built straight shed dating from 1853, an exceptionally early construction date, although its plain and functional design gave little away to indicate its age. It had a transverse pitched roof, originally slated, but had been replaced in 1957 with one of tightly overlaid corrugated iron. Eight lines of three smoke ventilators were positioned in the roof above each of the Shed's stabling roads. The shed building was not particularly long, with each road only capable of holding under cover two large tender engines or four tank engines. There was, however, room for several further engines on each road at the front of the Shed, where three water columns were to be found evenly spaced between the running lines. Serviced engines would be found lined up, coaled and watered here, ready for their next turn of duty. Quite often a shed visit coincided with a set of footplate men, oil cans in hand, making final preparations for an engine's departure. This could often be accompanied by the familiar explosive sound of the locomotive safety valve blowing steam skywards.

A large coaling stage dominated the scene on the far side of the shed yard, set against rising ground that formed the boundary with Bulmer's Cider Factory. Several of the Bulmer boys were at school with me at the time. A highlevel footpath ran behind the boundary fence, running along the top of the bank the full length of the shed site, squeezed between the railway boundary and the cider factory wall. This was a favoured viewing point for enthusiasts checking on latest arrivals at the Shed. The coaling stage of typical GWR design dated from around 1921. It was topped with a large water tank, internally divided into two sections with a capacity of 35,000 gallons of hard and 38,000 gallons of soft water. This supplied the Shed's six water columns around the complex. Three were positioned between the eight shed roads, a further one conveniently placed between the coaling stage and the turntable, and two

Hereford Shed showing the eight-road stone-built building, with its transverse pitched roof and smoke ventilators, in the early 1960s. From the left is a tender-facing Hall 5MT 4-6-0, 8F 2-8-0 No. 3816, 5MT 4-6-0 No. 4930 *Hagley Hall* followed by another tender-facing Hall 4-6-0. Then there is Worcester's No. 7920 *Coney Hall*, with A03 chalked on the smokebox door from a previous working, and yet another Hall 4-6-0. Typically, these were mostly visiting engines, which often outnumbered Hereford's home fleet in the middle of the day. M. HALE/GREAT WESTERN TRUST

HEREFORD ENGINE SHED

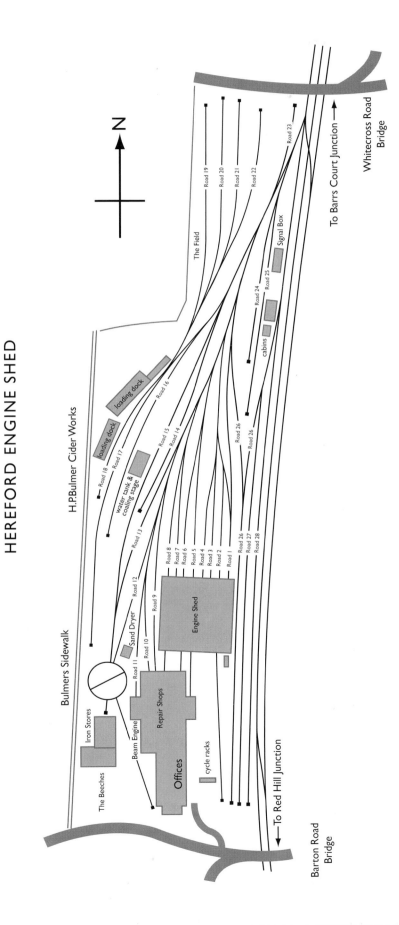

The Beeches

Iron Stores

Bulmers Sidewalk

H.P.Bulmer Cider Works

Beam Engine

Offices

Repair Shops

cycle racks

Sand Dryer

Road 11

Road 10

Road 9

Road 12

Engine Shed

Road 8
Road 7
Road 6
Road 5
Road 4
Road 3
Road 2
Road 1

Road 26
Road 27
Road 28

To Red Hill Junction

Barton Road Bridge

Road 13

water tank & coaling stage

Road 18
Road 17

loading dock

loading dock

Road 16

Road 15
Road 14

Road 26

Road 26

cabins

Road 24
Road 25

Signal Box

Road 23

Road 19
Road 20
Road 21
Road 22

The Field

To Barrs Court Junction

Whitecross Road Bridge

N

RICHARD SODDY

adjacent to the up and down running lines for passing freight trains. The coaling stage was serviced by an elevated ramp known as No. 16 road, whilst Nos. 17 to 22 behind and to the north of the coaling stage were for Bulmer's Cider rail traffic. These had restricted access due to curvature and were shunted by the Barton freight yard pilot, which for these access reasons was always a smaller Hawksworth 2F 1600 0-6-0PT.

The coaling stage No. 15 road was the first port of call for engines coming onto shed and was where disposal and servicing also took place. On late weekday afternoons, when my shed visits often occurred, a long line of engines would build up there awaiting servicing. These would be a combination of home-based engines after their day's work and foreign visitors, mostly off main-line freight workings. The most interesting of the regular daily arrivals were two Llanelly Stanier 8F 48000 2-8-0s. These were off freight services from Llandilo Junction, which were routed via Jersey Marine (reverse) and the Vale of Neath line to Aberdare and Pontypool Road. Other regular arrivals would include two and sometimes three Shrewsbury engines off inwards freight workings. A pit ran under the coaling stage road for part of its length to facilitate underside locomotive access, whilst deep piles of ash were scattered untidily all around. Alongside was stop-blocked No. 14 siding, where steel-lined wagons for ash loading, and later a mechanical crane to facilitate this, might be found.

The shed layout had a logical flow to allow engines to freely move sequentially through the servicing and preparation process. When coaling was completed they could take water if necessary and then move forward onto the Shed's 65ft. Ransome and Rapier turntable, dating from 1908, located in the yard's south-west corner. From there, the turned engines proceeded via No. 13 road to the front of the Shed for stabling, ready for their next duty. Fortunately, due to the Depot's rather remote location from the main passenger station, a second 65ft. Ransome and Rapier 1912 turntable was located there. This, or the Brecon Curve triangle, would be used for turning engines off terminating short turn round passenger services.

The four-road repair shop was situated slightly offset and to the rear of the Shed. Locomotive repairs were also carried out in the open on No. 5 road. This extended out of the rear of the main shed onto a short siding beside the repair shop and had a pit to assist underside locomotive access. It also contained a mechanical hoist for lifting engines for axle-box repairs. Some repair work also occurred on No. 9 road alongside the north wall of the Shed; the siding also providing access to the repair shops. The latter was a well-equipped facility able to deal with a wide range of locomotive repairs. It seemed to see more than its fair share of work due to Hereford's strategic position midway along the North & West route, being the place where ailing engines seemed to limp into for replacement. This inevitably resulted in unexpected foreign engines being stood alongside the shed wall for lengthy periods awaiting assessment, spares or, particularly latterly, a possible condemnation decision.

Smaller buildings were to be found on the south-west corner of the site, well away from the main line. These included a small stores building beyond the turntable, a beam engine house for lifting water and a sand dryer. Further stores and a staff mess room were located within the repair shop. A railway-owned house, *The Beeches*, stood on railway land between the turntable and the main road and would have been occupied by a senior staff member.

With the focus so often in railway histories being on the locomotives, the large resident human workforce necessary to enable a steam shed to function is often passed by. From a faded notebook, we know that in 1960, George Bretherton was the Shed Master and Messrs. Trotman, Steele and Parry the Shift Running Foremen. The latter trio had the day to day responsibility for booking-on and matching the depot's and visiting footplate crews to their duties, as well as the allocation of locomotives to diagrammed turns in conjunction with District Locomotive Control. On the locomotive maintenance side, Mechanical

1959/60 Hereford Shed
Locomotive Allocation and Staffing

Locomotive Allocation December 1959			Mechanical Staff – January 1960		
Class	**Diagrams**	**Allocation**	**Staffing**	**Planning**	**Actual**
HEREFORD			Chargeman Bennett	1	1
Hall 4-6-0s	2	3	Fitters	10	10
4300 2-6-0s	1	4	Fitters Mates	9	9
2251 0-6-0s	4	5	Electrician	1	1
78000 2-6-0	1	1	Boilersmiths	2	2
4200 2-8-0T	1.5	2 plus 1 loan	Boilersmiths Mates	2	1
5101 2-6-2T	1	1	Coppersmiths	0	0
5700 0-6-0PTs	7.5	10	Blacksmiths	0	0
7400 0-6-0PTs	0	1	Mechanical Apprentices	2	2
1600 0-6-0PTs	5	4	Boiler Apprentice	1	1
LEOMINSTER			**Total**	**28**	**27**
7400 0-6-0PTs	1	1			
1400 0-4-2Ts	1	1			
Total	**25**	**34**	**Shed Staff – January 1960**		
			Staffing	**Planning**	**Actual**
Salaried Staff - January 1960			Shed Chargeman	2	2
Shed Master:	George Bretherton		Chargeman Engine Cleaner	1	1
Shift Foremen:	Bert Trotman		Steam Raisers	3	2
	Tom Steele		Coalmen	3	3
	Les Parry		Fire Droppers	4	3
Chief Clerk:	Mr Bubb		Boiler Washers	3	2
Clerical Staff:	Cyril Walling (Rosters)		Stores Issuers	3	2
	Mary James		Tube Cleaners	2	2
	Miss Walker		Leading Shedman	1	1
	and 3 others.		Shedmen	8	6
Total	**11**		**Total**	**30**	**24**

From the handwritten notebook of George Bartlett, newly-appointed District Running and Maintenance Officer, Gloucester. His responsibility would last only a few months until the shed was transferred to the Newport Motive Power District. There are some inconsistencies here – Leominster's sub-shed's allocation is listed separately, but Ledbury's 1.5 x class 4200 and Ross-on-Wye's 1 x freight trip diagrams are shown within the main Hereford numbers. No information was recorded on drivers, firemen or engine cleaners.

Chargeman Bennett controlled twenty-seven fitters, boiler smiths and electricians whilst the Shed Chargeman was responsible for thirty steam raisers, fire droppers, boiler washers, stores issuers, shed men and coal men. In the office under the watchful eye of the Chief Clerk, Mr. Bubb, were a small team of administration, paybill and roster clerks. That resident shed workforce in 1959/60 was sixty-nine, of which seven were vacancies. The vacancies were mainly in the least attractive and poorest-paid duties of shed men, fire droppers and boiler washers. The depot establishment for footplate staff was not shown, but a former driver recalls there being about 110 drivers and 90 firemen. This gave a total workforce under the Shed Master's control of around 269 staff, a significant number for what was a moderate-sized shed. When you add separately managed traffic department staff at the passenger station and freight yards, which including passenger and freight guards, plus engineering staff to this total, it is clear that the railway was a significant employer in Hereford at this time.

Footplate route knowledge was a valued and important commodity which became more comprehensive as a driver progressed through the depot link structure. The links, as they were called, divided the Depot's varied train crew workload into more manageable chunks. Drivers and fireman might progress from the junior links, covering shunting, to local freight or passenger, and then longer-distance freight and passenger work. At some depots, duties would be mixed within the link, either to equalise earnings or to more efficiently retain depot route knowledge. There would also be a shed link of medically-restricted drivers.

A long-retired Hereford driver recalled his route knowledge acquired as being to Cardiff, Bristol, Shrewsbury, Crewe, Gloucester, Worcester, Birmingham Snow Hill, Brecon and Dowlais via Three Cocks Junction, as well as a 'double-home' turn, involving staying away overnight, to Llanelly via the Vale of Neath line. Other retired Hereford drivers confirm they regularly worked this 'double home turn' almost to the end of steam. Motive power was a returning Llanelly Stanier 8F 2-8-0. Some crews also signed the Ross-on-Wye to Lydbrook (former Monmouth) branch line and the Leominster to Kington branch after the Leominster sub-shed closed. The most interesting omission is not signing beyond Worcester towards Oxford and Paddington. Hereford men would also relieve at the sub-sheds when cover was required. This is not necessarily a definitive route knowledge list, but does give a valuable insight into the knowledge held by experienced Hereford footplate staff.

Hereford as a main depot was also responsible at different times during the period 1958-1964 for the small sub-sheds at Craven Arms, Ledbury, Leominster and Ross-on-Wye. The story of these and their out-based allocations are told in later chapters.

Hereford Driver Gilbert Howls is wished well on his retirement by fellow footplate man Joe Mason in 1958. Driver Howls looks quite a character and an experienced old hand. No. 6992 *Arborfield Hall* in the background is looking very clean and had returned from a Heavy General overhaul at Swindon Works on 29 January 1958. KIDDERMINSTER RAILWAY MUSEUM

Hereford driver Bill Ingram, with traditional pocket watch and chain, completes his final turn of duty before retirement in 1959 with No. 6916 *Misterton Hall* his final steed. Fireman John Davies, who would later become a long-serving Hereford driver, is in the background. JOHN DAVIES

Footplate and shunting staff, around 1955, at Hereford including, on the left, driver Ron Wargen and, far right, driver Fred Foster. Senior time server by far is 3F 5700 0-6-0PT No. 3728, built in 1937 and a Hereford engine since March 1938. An ex-GWR shunting truck completes the scene. CHRIS MARTIN

An ex-GWR auto coach body at the rear of the shed site behind the turntable on 6 May 1962. It has found a new use for the Depot's Mutual Improvement Classes where senior drivers give their time voluntarily to pass on knowledge to firemen and passed-firemen in particular. Official records consulted in preparation for this book confirm auto-coach body W177W was sent to Hereford for this purpose in October 1961. JOHN RUMSEY

Depot Mutual Improvement Class with Hereford footplate staff L-R Jack Cornes, Charlie Smallwood, John Gooding (that year Mayor of Hereford), Keith Harris, Layton Roberts, John Davies, Jimmy Collier, Alf Ledbury and Robin Jones. Taken in around 1956, Pontypool Road's 5MT 4-6-0 No. 6812 *Chesford Grange* is also featured. JOHN DAVIES

Hymek diesel training in 1963 with Hereford drivers L-R Ron Wargen, Grenville Wargen, Fred Oldman, Jack Cornes, an unknown trainee and Vic Thomas. This was probably linked to the Hymeks' initial introduction on Hereford to Paddington services. CHRIS MARTIN

Back of the Shed viewed from high up on the Barton Road Bridge, from where the access road dropped steeply down. The repair shops are on the left with the main loco shed building behind. On 21 August 1963, lined up are Nos. 7446 and 7437 (both in store), 9665, 9717 and 5092 (all withdrawn), and 1458 (in store). A withdrawn Hall 4-6-0 is standing beside the repair shop. Keith Fairey/Colour-Rail.com

Hereford Shed scene on Saturday, 18 August 1962. A local 5700 0-6-0PT pokes its nose out of the shed alongside 8F 2-8-0 No. 3841 of Pontypool Road. Of most interest is Carlisle Upperby's 7P Royal Scot 4-6-0 No. 46118 *Royal Welch Fusilier,* which from its LMR-style head code board has earlier worked in an inter-regional parcels or pigeon special. R.C. Riley/Transport Treasury

Side view of the shed front on 2 January 1964, showing up well its substantial stone built construction and 1957 replacement roof. Pictured 1P 0-4-2T No. 1458 had arrived in July 1963 from Oswestry, but was initially placed in store until later used for working the Kington branch freight. 4MT 2-6-2T No. 5154 had arrived from Gloucester in April 1963 to work Gloucester branch passenger services, but had been a condition-led withdrawal in August 1963 and now awaited scrap yard disposal. R.G. Nelson/Terry Walsh collection

Good modellers' detail of the Shed's side wall with its interesting inlaid arch on 19 April 1964. Old Oak Common's filthy 5MT 4-6-0 No. 4962 *Ragley Hall* is stabled on the road usually kept for failed engines and, indeed, it did not move from here for several weeks. Michael Jennings

Panoramic shed yard view on 22 April 1964, with No. 15 road from the coaling stage to the left, then stop-blocked No. 14 road disappearing under locomotive ash and, alongside that, No. 13 engine release road which contains a servicing pit. Several engines are undergoing coaling, whilst Old Oak Common's No. 4962 *Ragley Hall* is partially in view on the shed side and Gloucester's 4MT 2-6-0 No. 7307 has steam up ready to work the 2.43pm passenger train to Gloucester. R.G. Nelson/Terry Walsh collection

The coaling stage in close up with a Stanier 8F 2-8-0 probably from Llanelly or Shrewsbury, whilst Hereford's 3MT 0-6-0 No. 2287 and another 2251 0-6-0 just in view also wait to be coaled. Engine disposal took place on the same road and piles of ash lie around in typical untidy fashion. The massive roof-topped water tank is also shown to good effect. Roy Palmer

Looking north towards the coaling stage. 4MT 2-6-2T No. 4575 is a rare migratory bird calling in at Hereford on 12 June 1960. It is moving towards the turntable behind the photographer and will then return back towards the right to stable at the shed front. A Bristol Bath Road engine until that week, it was on a depot transfer move via the Severn Tunnel, Hereford and Shrewsbury to Machynlleth, where it would spend the summer working on the Cambrian Coast. JOHN GOSS

Shed snow plough standby over the Christmas/New Year period has been 3MT 0-6-0 No. 2286, seen on 2 January 1964 standing in front of the repair shop. The snow plough fitment required the removal of the buffers; the left-hand one lying on the ground nearby. R.G. NELSON/TERRY WALSH COLLECTION

Nos. 9 and 10 roads beside the Shed with the closed doors of the repair shop in the background. Shrewsbury's 5MT 4-6-0 No. 7821 *Ditcheat Manor* is in steam standing on No. 10 road on 29 April 1961. Behind, on No. 9 road, is Llanelly's 8F 2-8-0 No. 48707 off a freight train from Llandilo Junction, via the Vale of Neath line. No. 9 road is where failed engines were often stabled and all may not be well with this Llanelly engine. RON HERBERT

Inside the repair shop on 27 April 1964, Hereford's newly-allocated 7P Castle 4-6-0 No. 5056 *Earl of Powis* is receiving attention to the right-hand cylinder with three repair staff in attendance. It had recently been transferred from Cardiff East Dock, arriving working a freight train from South Wales on 6 April 1964. It had been failed on arrival and would remain under repair until 1 June 1964, although it then did some useful work. R.G. Nelson/Terry Walsh collection

More repairs being undertaken on 20 November 1963, with machinery and metal work criss-crossing the scene. Withdrawn, but appropriately named 6MT 4-6-0 No. 1017 *County of Hereford* is being made fit to travel to Ward's Scrap Yard, Sheffield, almost a year after withdrawal from Shrewsbury. It had spent many months with five other withdrawn engines stored at Craven Arms and all had unexpectedly appeared together at Hereford to be made fit to travel to their ultimate destination. R.G. Nelson/Terry Walsh collection

Whilst the 5205s were equally capable of, and possibly did participate in, main-line freight train work, their primary role here was banking duties at Ledbury where they assisted freight trains from South Wales to the West Midlands. One engine was out-based there all week, booked light engine from Hereford on Monday mornings, and returned after the last freight train had passed in the early hours of Sunday morning. The Ledbury sub-shed and banking duties are more fully described in a later chapter.

Collett 4MT 5101 and BR Standard 3MT 82000 2-6-2Ts

The 5101 2-6-2Ts were powerful and versatile engines that served Hereford well from the arrival of the first, No. 5156, in November 1957 up to Shed closure. There was only one class member on the allocation until February 1962, although three different engines were involved during that period. From that date, Hereford lost its last 4MT 4300 2-6-0 and a second Prairie tank arrived as replacement. This put together the two best-remembered engines at the Depot, Nos. 4115 and 4135. In August 1962, there was a significant change when two BR Standard 3MT 82000 2-6-2Ts, Nos. 82001 and 82002, were brought in from distant Templecombe. Consequentially, that September No. 4115 went into store, whilst No. 4135 continued to work alongside the new arrivals. No. 4115 spent that dreadful 1962/63 winter snow covered in freezing conditions, stored on the stop blocks outside the rear of the shed. It, however, lived to fight another day, being seen in steam on 13 February 1963 and shortly afterwards leaving for its new depot, Severn Tunnel Junction. A born survivor, it was given a general overhaul at Swindon Works in June 1963

No. 4107 on shed at Hereford on 26 April 1964, demonstrating well the elegant lines of these powerful and versatile engines. Their role here was exclusively on Gloucester branch passenger services. No. 4107 was a September 1935 build and a late arrival at Hereford in September 1963 from Neyland, working up to branch and depot closure when it was re-allocated to Severn Tunnel Junction.
MANCHESTER LOCOMOTIVE SOCIETY COLLECTION

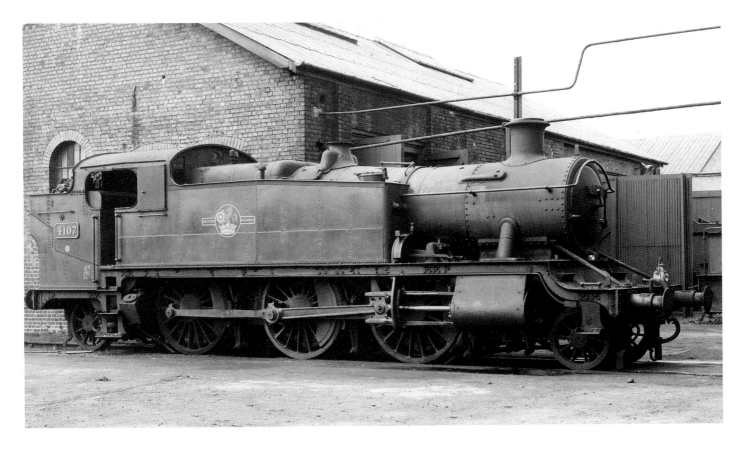

No. 4115 was a regular Hereford engine, entering service in October 1936 before arriving from Newton Abbot in November 1958 and working continuously until September 1962. It then went into store, pushed out by the arrival of BR Standard 3MT 2-6-2Ts, until a new life at Severn Tunnel Junction beckoned the following year. R.H.G. SIMPSON

No. 4135, another Hereford regular, is seen on shed here on 26 April 1964. An October 1939 build, it arrived from Pontypool Road in February 1962, working until condition-led withdrawal in June 1964, when it was replaced by No. 4157 from Pontypool Road. MANCHESTER LOCOMOTIVE SOCIETY

No. 5154 caught in late autumn sunshine beside the Shed on 20 November 1963. An older class member built in February 1930, it arrived at Hereford in April 1963 from store at Cheltenham, replacing BR Standard 3MT 2-6-2Ts on Gloucester passenger services. Still displaying a faded cycling lion crest, it clearly had not had a full overhaul and re-paint since the 1950s. The engine became a condition-led withdrawal in August 1963. R.G. Nelson/Terry Walsh collection

No. 82001 and sister engine 82002 arrived at Hereford in August 1962 from Templecombe to replace 5101 2-6-2Ts on Gloucester passenger services. Their reign was short, moving on in April 1963 when traditional order was restored. Pictured on 23 March 1963 at the rear of the Shed with 0-6-0PT No. 9717 in partial view, the latter withdrawn in December 1962. John Goss

No. 82002, taken on 21 April 1963 shortly before re-allocation to Exmouth Junction. It is standing on Road No. 5 which extended out of the back of the Shed by the Repair Shops. Discarded oil drums are prominent in the foreground. MICHAEL JENNINGS

and would continue to work banking freight trains through the Severn Tunnel until its June 1965 withdrawal.

After eight months, ex-GWR order was restored, and in April 1963 Nos. 82001 and 82002 returned westwards to Exmouth Junction. Replacements Nos. 4161 and 5154 arrived from Cheltenham, both having been in store there since October 1962. This made three operational 5101 2-6-2Ts – Nos. 4135, 4161 and 5154 – this number remaining until Depot closure. Individual engines did change, but only driven by condition-led withdrawals with replacements

immediately provided. The final three at Depot closure were Nos. 4107, 4157 and 4161. All found new homes, with the first two heading for Severn Tunnel Junction, the last to Worcester.

Both the 5101s and 82000s were specifically used for working Hereford-Gloucester passenger services. Two were required to be working each day on multiple round trips. The powerful and elegant 5101 2-6-2Ts proved a great asset to the Depot and are fondly remembered as an important part of the Hereford railway scene.

Collett 3MT 2251 0-6-0s and BR Standard 2MT 78000 2-6-0

The 3MT 2251 0-6-0 tender engines were arguably the most useful and versatile locomotives on Hereford's allocation. Mainly there for local freight work and spare cover, they were the Shed Running Foreman's first fall-back choice for Gloucester passenger duties when a 4MT 5101 2-6-2T wasn't available. They were also the standby for the Depot's BR Standard 2MT 78000 on the Brecon branch freight trip and yet again capable of interchange with 3F 5700 0-6-0PTs on certain of their local freight trips. Versatile as ever, No. 2286 was on special standby duties attached to the Depot's snowplough over the 1963/64 Christmas and New Year period. They were also ideal to work the Depot breakdown train when called out and for weekend engineering work, ballast or spoil trains. They were also used double-heading special trains over the weight-restricted Brecon branch, with Hereford's Nos. 2242 and 2249 taking over a lengthy Newcastle-upon-Tyne to Sennybridge troop train at Hereford on 24 May 1959.

When Craven Arms ceased to be a Shrewsbury sub-shed in January 1963, due to LMR/WR regional boundary changes, responsibility passed to Hereford. This now included a Hereford 3MT 2251 0-6-0 to be out-based there for Knighton banking duties.

In June 1958, there were five 2251s on the allocation and whilst individual engines changed, roundly that number remained operational for the next few years. There then came a downturn when, from October 1962, only two were in use with two more in store. Matters improved that December, when

No. 2241 looks sparklingly clean, although filled with the dreaded ovoid coal, on Shed in 1961. A war baby, it entered service in March 1945, arriving at Hereford in May 1958. Except for a one-month possible paper transfer to Exmouth Junction in July 1963, it worked locally until its February 1964 withdrawal. It received a Heavy Intermediate overhaul at Caerphilly Works in March 1961, explaining its pristine condition. JOHN GOSS

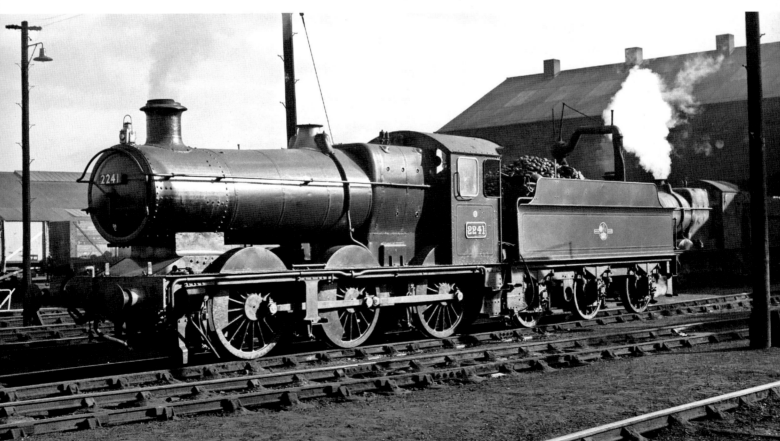

No. 2242 outside the back of the Shed on 22 April 1964 with 0-4-2T No. 1458 just poking its nose out behind. The 2251s were versatile engines ideally suited to the Depot's local freight and passenger work. An April 1945 build, No. 2242 worked here from July 1957 to Shed closure when it transferred to Gloucester. R.G. Nelson/Terry Walsh collection

Nos. 2249 and 2286, fellow shed mates, meet and exchange pleasantries at Ludlow on 14 April 1963. No.2286 is bringing a trip from Craven Arms into the down sidings whilst No. 2249 is standing on the up main waiting to proceed tender first towards Craven Arms, possibly as an exchange loco from Hereford for the 2251 on the Knighton banking duty. Nick Nicholson/Transport Treasury

No. 1455 on Shed at Hereford on 16 October 1955. Built in July 1935, it had worked locally since June 1941, leaving with No. 1445 for Banbury in August 1961, following withdrawal of the Tenbury Wells auto-service. JOHN HODGE

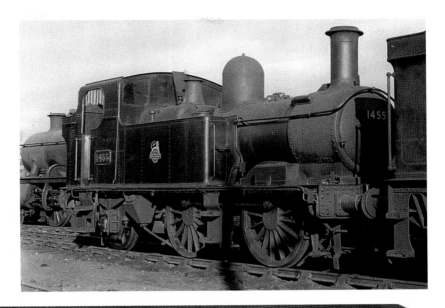

No. 6438 standing at the side of the Shed in 1961, was a short-term transfer from Abercynon between December 1960 and February 1961. Initially an unexplained transfer, it mirrored a period when Hereford's 0-4-2T No. 1445 was at Wolverhampton Works for overhaul. Whether it was ever used on the Tenbury Wells auto-service is not known. JOHN GOSS

No. 7401 in 1959, standing beside Hereford's repair shop in a position usually reserved for stored engines. Entering traffic in August 1936, it was only based at Hereford between January and its June 1959 withdrawal, and appears unlikely to work again. JOHN GOSS

No. 7418, standing outside the back of the Shed on 29 April 1961, looks in fine shape and recently returned from works overhaul. It arrived at Hereford in July 1959 from Swindon, moving on to Croes Newydd in February 1962, displaced from the Kington branch freight trip by 1400 0-4-2Ts. RON HERBERT

No. 7437 in store in the familiar position beside the Repair Shops in 1962/63. A wag had chalked 'For Sale £1 or nearest offer'. The offer was eventually taken up by Llanelly Shed in December 1963 after almost two years in store. Hereford cathedral's imposing tower can be seen in the distance. JOHN GOSS

Locomotive Allocations and Workload Overview

Having looked class by class at Hereford's locomotive allocation, we'll now focus on how overall locomotive numbers changed over the years along with the principal reasons. Sample allocations at specific dates are shown here with further examples in the appendices.

In February 1958, there were forty-four engines based here, with all but one of GWR design, although some had been built post-nationalisation. The February 1958 allocation comprised eight Hall 5MT 4-6-0s; one Manor 5MT 4-6-0; two 5205 8F 2-8-0Ts; six 4300 4MT 2-6-0s; six 2251 3MT 0-6-0s; one 5101 4MT 2-6-2T; nine 5700 3F 0-6-0PTs; two 7400 2F 0-6-0PTs; five 1600 2F 0-6-0PTs; three 1400 1P 0-4-2Ts and one BR Standard 78000 2MT 2-6-0. However, storm clouds were gathering, and within months there would be significant changes to the Depot's workload and allocation. This fell by almost 20 per cent from forty-four to thirty-six during the next year, with most of that reduction being in larger main-line locomotives. These changes pre-dated the days of

mass locomotive withdrawals and almost all were transferred elsewhere, with only two condition-led withdrawals occurring during the year. The losses were a direct result of the summer 1958 timetable change described more fully in the Halls section of Chapter Two. Indeed, their numbers were down from eight to only three engines by February 1959, whilst the single Manor had also gone and the 4MT 4300s were down from six to just three engines. This work loss did ultimately have a hidden benefit for the Depot, in that it would remain relatively protected from the progressive dieselisation of longer-distance passenger and later freight services. Branch passenger, local freight and yard shunting work in, which the Depot's engines remained an exclusive steam activity almost up to Depot closure. In reality, even these duties did not have a long-term future and it was inevitable that eventually they would disappear. Meanwhile a reduced allocation of 5MT Hall and latterly 7P Castle 4-6-0s would retain a small, but distinct foothold on main-line passenger work. Despite

Hereford Shed viewed from the northern end with the Hereford avoiding line in the foreground heading towards South Wales. The Depot coaling stage is prominent on the right-hand side with Bulmer's Cider Factory behind. An unidentified 5MT Hall 4-6-0 is shunting coal wagons off its train whilst a shunter standing on the up avoiding line leans on his shunting pole. Meanwhile, the Barton Sidings pilot, a 2F 1600 0-6-0PT, can be seen in the left background. BEN ASHWORTH

Hereford's loss of long-distance freight locomotive working, its footplate crews continued to relieve freight services en route to the North-West and the West Midlands. Likewise, Hereford drivers were DMU trained and continued to work the revamped Cardiff – Hereford – Birmingham semi-fast service.

Locomotive Allocation – February 1958 85C Hereford

Hall 5MT 4-6-0		5205 8F 2-8-0T		7400 2F 0-6-0PT	
4943 *Marrington Hall*		5226	5243	7416	7437
4975 *Umberslade Hall*		**2251 3MT 0-6-0**		**1600 2F 0-6-0PT**	
5977 *Beckford Hall*		2225	2266	1617	1662
5998 *Trevor Hall*		2242	2274	1625	1667
6916 *Misterton Hall*		2249	2295	1657	
6984 *Owsden Hall*		**5101 4MT 2-6-2T**		**1400 1P 0-4-2T**	
6989 *Wightwick Hall*		5156		1445	1456
6992 *Arborfield Hall*		**5700 3F 0-6-0PT**		1455	
Manor 5MT 4-6-0		3728	8781	**78000 2MT 2-6-0**	
7805 *Broome Manor*		4657	9619	78004	
4300 4MT 2-6-0		4678	9665	**Total: 44**	
5350	6359	5765	9717		
5377	7312	8701			
6326	7326 (9304)				

LOCOMOTIVE ALLOCATIONS AND WORKLOAD OVERVIEW • 67

One of the Halls, and later Castles, passenger diagrams on the North & West route was over twenty-eight hours long. Likewise, one of the freight shunting turns was a seventeen-hour duty and another a continuous twenty-four hours per day. The 82000 and later 5101 class 2-6-2Ts' two Gloucester branch diagrams involved one making two and the other three round trips to Gloucester daily. At the other end of the scale, the lone 78000 2-6-0 spent each day on the leisurely Brecon branch freight trip, leaving at 10am each morning and back home by 5pm. A lengthy diagram, however, was the 2251 0-6-0 on the 8.25am freight to Gloucester, shunting stations and byways en route, not getting to Gloucester until after 1pm. The engine then took a break on Gloucester Shed before bringing back the 6.35pm branch freight which, after similar leisurely progress, ran into Hereford at 11.20pm. After a few hours respite, it might be out again for the 8.25am the next morning.

A fascinating shed with a truly varied workload that is now, but a fading memory from over fifty years ago.

Visiting Locomotives on Shed

The Hereford Shed story could not be complete without looking at visiting locomotives. On weekday afternoons up to half of the engines to be seen could be foreign visitors, mostly gathered under the coaling stage, waiting servicing. As well as this varied collection, along the Shed side out of steam might be visitors which had failed in traffic and were awaiting repair.

Visiting Passenger and Parcels Engines

Visiting passenger engines tended to be few in number, as there weren't many terminating passenger services worked by foreign engines booked for lengthy turnarounds at Hereford or overnight stabling. Because of the Shed's remoteness from the station, engines on short turnarounds would turn via the Barrs Court triangle or on the turntable north of the station and await back workings in the station area. Nevertheless, there were a few regular passenger shed visitors and these changed little over the years.

Each morning, a Gloucester 4MT 4300 2-6-0 arrived on shed around 10am off the 5.10am Gloucester-Hereford branch freight. After a lengthy layover, it headed to the station to work the 2.43pm to Gloucester passenger service. The four-hour layover was too long for the inbound Gloucester crew to have stayed with their engine and a fresh Hereford or Gloucester crew must have worked the return service.

Also on Shed and waiting for a late afternoon departure would be a Worcester 5MT Hall, Grange or 4MT 75000 4-6-0. This would have arrived early morning on an inwards working from Worcester and left for the station to work the 5.40pm Hereford-Worcester local passenger service. Typically, Worcester's No. 6806 *Blackwell Grange* worked the service on 5 March and No. 7928 *Wolf Hall* on 28 May 1964.

Between 4 March and 1 May 1963, major bridgeworks restricted engine changing and turntable access at Shrewsbury, disrupting Manchester/Liverpool-Plymouth/South Wales express passenger services that would otherwise have changed from LMR to WR motive power there. For that short period, LMR engines worked through to Hereford or beyond, and this brought an unusual number of Longsight and Crewe passenger engines, as well as those

coming off northbound from Bristol and Cardiff, onto Shed for servicing.

In the winter 1963 timetable, and possibly in other years, an Old Oak Common 7P Castle 4-6-0 came on Shed off the last 7.15pm Paddington-Hereford, terminating at 11.5pm. It returned with an early-morning service to Paddington the next day. On Sunday, 17 November, Old Oak Common's No. 7035 *Ogmore Castle* was on Shed, having arrived late on the Saturday night. Some years a Worcester Castle might also make an overnight stay.

From time to time special passenger trains, and in particular troop trains, worked into the area, along with pigeon and parcels specials, some of these terminating or changing engines at Hereford. Unusual Shed visitors included Bristol Bath Road 7P 4-6-0 No.

7014 *Caerhays Castle* on 12 June 1960; Wolverhampton Stafford Road's No. 5031 *Totnes Castle* on 18 May 1963; Lancaster 6P/5F Crab 2-6-0 No. 42895 on 28 June 1959 and Crewe North Jubilee 4-6-0 No. 45556 *Nova Scotia* on 6 March 1962. From even further afield came Scottish Region 7P Britannia 4-6-2 No. 70051 *Firth of Forth* on 18 May 1962; Carlisle Upperby 7P Royal Scot 4-6-0 No. 46118 *Royal Welch Fusilier* on 18 August 1962 and Carlisle Kingmoor Black 5 No. 44878 on 9 May 1964.

Locomotive failures on through express services, their trains worked forward by the Hereford locomotive standby, would inevitably limp onto Shed for attention. Standing cold and lifeless one day in the early 1960s was Cardiff Canton 8P 4-6-0 No. 6018 *King Henry VI*, still rather embarrassingly carrying

BR Standard 7P 4-6-2 No. 70051 *Firth of Forth*, from distant Glasgow Corkerhill, unquestionably gets the prize as the Depot's most unexpected visitor I ever saw. I remember seeing it there on 18 May 1962. How it had got there remains a mystery, but it was most likely off a troop train or a pigeon special. In preparation for this book, I discovered John had seen it and photographed it as well. JOHN GOSS

4MT 2-6-0 No. 6394, a daily visiting Gloucester engine, is seen on Shed on 2 January 1964. It had arrived on the 5.10am branch freight from Gloucester mid-morning and is being prepared to work the 2.43pm passenger train home. Departure time is approaching and steam pressure has been raised, tender watering is underway and the driver is returning to his engine ready for departure. R.G. NELSON/ TERRY WALSH COLLECTION

its 1M68 headboard, indicating it had failed whilst working the 8.55am Cardiff-Manchester. Another sinner was Cardiff East Dock 7P Castle 4-6-0 No. 5092 *Tresco Abbey*, failing on the 12.5pm Manchester-Plymouth on 1 May 1963. It would never turn a wheel in anger again and was condemned on site. Crewe North 7P Royal Scot No. 46135 *The East Lancashire Regiment* was noted dead outside the repair shop on 6 May 1962, with one pair of driving wheels removed having clearly suffered a major defect. Official BR locomotive record cards show Bristol St Phillip's Marsh 6MT 4-6-0 No. 1005 *County of Devon* received an 'unclassified repair' at Hereford on 18 April 1962 and the same depot's No. 1024 *County of Pembroke* similarly on 10 July 1962.

Some of the most unusual and unexplained visitors were tank engines from far-flung depots which could not possibly have worked trains into the area. These often turned out to be en route to or from main works overhauls which, in the 1960s, were still taking place in addition to Swindon at Caerphilly, Oswestry and Wolverhampton. On

23 September 1962, Worcester's 4MT 2-6-2T No. 8104, in gleaming black ex-works livery, was on Shed and two days later Bristol St Phillip's Marsh 3MT BR Standard 82000 2-6-2T No. 82043 made a call. On 18 November 1962 Carmarthen's 4MT 2-6-2T No. 6114, also in ex-works condition, was noted en route from Wolverhampton Works back to Carmarthen. Yet again, on 31 January 1963, Bristol Barrow Road's 4MT 2-6-2T No. 4103 called into the Shed.

Occasionally such visitors might have been on inter-depot transfer moves en route to their new depots. Such an unexpected visitor was former Bristol Bath Road 4MT 2-6-2T No. 4575. It paused at Hereford for servicing and to await a fresh footplate crew on 12 June 1960 whilst heading for its new home at Machynlleth, having travelled from Bristol via the Severn Tunnel, Hereford and on to Shrewsbury. A tell-tale shiny empty semi-circle on the smokebox door, where the locomotive's shed plate should have been, was a clear indicator that this was a transfer movement.

7P 4-6-0 No. 7027 *Thornbury Castle* of Worcester complete with *Cathedrals Express* head-board is standing at the Shed front on Sunday, 13 May 1962. It had probably worked this service in from Paddington on Saturday evening and is standing down waiting its return working. Another Collett 4-6-0 is to its left whilst to its right is BR Standard 7P 4-6-2 No. 70015 *Apollo*. JOHN GOSS

4MT 2-6-0 No. 7307 of Gloucester, minus front and cab side number plates, is preparing to work the 2.43pm Hereford-Gloucester branch passenger train on 22 April 1964. Entering traffic in November 1921, it was unusually assembled at Swindon Works with parts manufactured by contractor Robert Stephenson and Co. Arriving at Gloucester in November 1963, it would be withdrawn just six weeks after the photograph was taken. R.G. NELSON/TERRY WALSH COLLECTION

8P 4-6-0 No. 6018
King Henry VI of Cardiff Canton is a rare visitor to Hereford sometime in 1961/62, seen here standing dead and lifeless on No. 9 road beside the Shed, which is where failed engines were usually found. The 1M68 head code suggests the engine had failed at Hereford whilst working the 8.55am Cardiff-Manchester. No. 6018 was a Cardiff Canton engine from September 1960 to June 1962; the 88A head code only applied after January 1961. JOHN GOSS

7P 4-6-0 No. 5093
Upton Castle, has been serviced and is ready for its next duty on 3 April 1960, having worked a 1X03 special in from the London area. A time-serving Old Oak Common engine, it was based there from December 1953 until its September 1963 withdrawal. Hereford's 3F 0-6-0PT No. 8787 sits in the background. A. WYCHERLEY/ KIDDERMINSTER RAILWAY MUSEUM

Visiting Freight Engines

Between thirty and forty long-distance freight trains passed through Hereford daily in each direction, and all remained steam hauled until well into 1964, within five months of Shed closure. A small number changed engines or terminated at Hereford and their engines would come onto Shed for servicing. Amongst these it was not unusual to find some from far-flung depots that had arrived off unscheduled freight train workings.

To illustrate, the following is an actual Shed visit made late afternoon on Friday, 17 January 1964. Of eighteen working locomotives there, eight were visitors. These comprised Llanelly 8F 2-8-0s Nos.48419 and 48732; Neath 5MT 4-6-0 No. 6867 *Peterston Grange*; Shrewsbury 8F 2-8-0s Nos.48020 and 48738; Shrewsbury 5MT 4-6-0 No. 7800 *Torquay Manor*; Worcester 5MT 4-6-0 No. 6856 *Stowe Grange;* and Worcester's BR Standard 4-6-0 No. 75025. Demonstrating the regularity of these callers, a

similarly-timed visit the following Friday, 24 January 1964 produced a slightly enhanced twenty-two working locomotives on Shed of which ten were from other depots. These were Llanelly 8F 2-8-0s Nos.48419 and 48525; Duffryn Yard 5MT No. 6987 *Shervington Hall*; Shrewsbury 8F 2-8-0 No. 48436 and 5MT 4-6-0 No. 7801 *Anthony Manor*; Banbury 8F 2-8-0 No. 3809; Cardiff East Dock 5MT No. 5952 *Cogan Hall*; Exeter 5MT No. 5967 *Bickmarsh Hall* and Pontypool Road 4MT 4300 2-6-0 No. 6338.

The regular daily afternoon presence of two Llanelly 8F 2-8-0s might surprise some readers. These arrived with lengthy freight trains from Llanelly's Llandilo Junction Yard, routed via Jersey Marine (reverse) and the Vale of Neath line to Aberdare and Pontypool Road. The single Neath or Duffryn Yard Hall or Grange 4-6-0 were also regular visitors working similar services from Margam via the Vale of Neath line and Pontypool Road.

4MT 2-6-0 No. 7322 is being moved around the Shed yard in 1961. It was a Severn Tunnel Junction engine from October 1957 to June 1961, then briefly transferred to Aberdare before moving on to Gloucester in August 1961. It was ultimately withdrawn from there in November 1961. The fact that the engine is carrying a local passenger head code suggests a Gloucester branch passenger working. It may be that it is now a Gloucester engine, although still carrying its former Severn Tunnel Junction shed plate. JOHN GOSS

Two of the three daily Shrewsbury 8F 2-8-0s were off Shrewsbury-Hereford pick-up freights that took almost half a day to complete their journey. They berthed and shunted traffic en route at Craven Arms, Woofferton, Ludlow, Leominster and Moreton-on-Lugg MOD Depot. When a third Shrewsbury 8F 2-8-0 was on shed, it came off a Shrewsbury-South Wales long-distance freight train. In the very early 1960s, one of the Shrewsbury pick-up freights might have a Churchward 4MT 4300 2-6-0, but latterly it would be more likely to have produced a 5MT Manor 4-6-0 or BR Standard 80000 4MT 2-6-4T.

The Worcester engine seen would be for the previously-described 5.40pm Hereford-Worcester passenger service. The additional Worcester engine may have come off a West Midlands-South Wales freight train whilst the remaining Banbury, Cardiff East Dock and Pontypool Road visitors were typical of unbalanced workings awaiting control orders home. Banbury engines seemingly far from home worked in via the West Midlands or may have been borrowed by Shrewsbury, where it is known a Banbury freight engine had a long layover. Examples included Banbury's 8F 2-8-0 No. 3826 on shed on 23 March 1963; No. 3809 on 24 January 1964; and Stanier 8F 2-8-0 No. 48417 on 23 June 1963. The Exeter 5MT Hall 4-6-0 was typical of inexplicable visitors that could appear from time to time.

Unscheduled visitors could equally be from far-flung LMR depots and would usually also have found their way to Hereford on unscheduled freight train workings. I can recall during the early 1960s, when there was a South Wales coal strike, numerous block trains of coal from North-West collieries passed through Hereford hauled by locomotives from a variety of Lancashire depots.

Typical unexplained visitors over the years included Wellingborough 8F 2-8-0 No. 48027 on 26 October 1962; Newton Heath WD 2-8-0 No. 90291 on 18 January 1963; Patricroft 8F 2-8-0 No. 48720 on 13 February 1963; Lancaster Green Ayre WD 2-8-0 No. 90316 on 11 May 1963 and Woodford Halse WD 2-8-0 No. 90237 on 9 July 1963. Hereford could certainly, from time to time, turn up some unusual visitors.

Such engines could occasionally come in small packages. An unexpected arrival on 27 November 1960 was the diminutive 1908-built ex-Swansea Harbour Trust Peckett 0-4-0ST No.1143. It was seen stabled beside the Shed having been withdrawn from Shrewsbury's Clee Hill sub-shed earlier that month. Clee Hill Quarry incline and sidings had closed several months earlier. I subsequently found out that No.1143 was en route from Shrewsbury to Caerphilly Works for scrapping. An equally unusual visitor was ex-L&Y 0-4-0ST No.51218 on 1 May 1963. It was making the long journey from home depot Swansea East Dock to Horwich Works for overhaul. I later learnt that after this was completed it had a disastrous journey back, such a small engine being clearly unsuited for long-distance main-line running. It had barely started back from Horwich Works on 1 July, formed next to the engine on a freight train, when it developed a hot box and was detached at Bury. From there it was taken to Bolton Shed for repairs. In the weeks that followed it was reported developing further hot boxes at Shrewsbury and Severn Tunnel Junction, whilst it was also seen on a low-loader wagon at Shrewsbury on 1 September 1963. Many months later it did get back to Swansea East Dock, but one wonders if there ought to have been a better way to move and overhaul such a small engine, usually confined to dock shunting.

Stanier 8F 2-8-0 No.48417 of Stourbridge Junction has clearly recently been out-shopped from main works. It will have worked in on a West Midlands to South Wales freight train. The engine is in light steam on Sunday, 23 June 1963 and a Hereford 3MT 2251 0-6-0 has shunted it across the yard. JOHN GOSS

Churchward 8F 2-8-0 No.2839 of Pontypool Road stabled out of steam on No. 9 road beside the Shed on Sunday, 13 May 1962. It had entered service in October 1912; these engines appeared somewhat dated alongside more recent designs. They were, however, powerful and well-liked engines, and No. 2839 would continue to work out of Pontypool Road for another two years until withdrawal in June 1964. JOHN GOSS

5MT 0-6-2T No. 6675 of Pontypool Road is an unusual visitor to Hereford on Friday, 18 May 1962. Of even greater interest is Crewe North 7P Royal Scot 4-6-0 No. 46135 *The East Lancashire Regiment* sitting forlornly minus a leading pair of driving wheels. It had been in this immovable state for at least a fortnight having clearly suffered a major defect. JOHN GOSS

5MT 4-6-0 No. 7827 *Lydham Manor* standing centre stage in a busy Shed scene on 2 January 1964. A Machynlleth engine, it may have been borrowed whilst on shed at Shrewsbury for one of their turns to Hereford. Alongside is Gloucester's 4MT 2-6-0 No. 6394. R.G. NELSON/TERRY WALSH COLLECTION

6P/5F Jubilee 4-6-0 No. 45660 *Rooke* is being shunted at Hereford in this undated scene. No. 45660 is carrying a Bristol Barrow Road shed plate and was transferred to Shrewsbury from there in September 1961. It is here most likely to have already been working from Shrewsbury, having been recently transferred there, or might even be on its actual transfer move from Bristol to Shrewsbury via the Severn Tunnel and Hereford. JOHN GOSS

8F 2-8-0 No. 48524 joins a short line of locomotives on Hereford's coaling stage road for servicing on Friday, 18 May 1962. A Llanelly engine, it would have worked in on a freight train from Llandilo Junction, via Jersey Marine (reverse), the Vale of Neath line and Pontypool Road. JOHN GOSS

Ex-Swansea Harbour Trust Peckett 0-4-0ST No. 1143 caused quite a stir when seen at Hereford on 27 November 1960, where it sits basking in the late autumn sun. It had recently been withdrawn from Shrewsbury's sub-shed at Clee Hill following closure of the Clee Hill Quarry railway. Built in 1906, it worked on Swansea Docks until December 1959 when it had been transferred to Clee Hill and was surprisingly still carrying its former Danygraig shed plate. My faded 1960 teenage diary excitedly recorded its presence whilst, fifty-six years later, John Goss was able to produce a photograph from the same day recording the scene. JOHN GOSS

HEREFORD SHUNTING ENGINE TURNS
SUMMER 1961 TIMETABLE

Pilot No.	Location	Times	Duties
1	Barrs Court Downside	6.15am-4am 21hr 45min	Shunts Barrs Court Downside. Also shunts Upside 2am-4am.
2	Barrs Court Upside	7am-9.20am 2hr 20min	6.55am light engine off shed to Barrs Court. Shunts Upside Yard then works 9.20am freight trip to Pontrilas.
2a		9.35am-12.55pm 3hrs 20mins	9.30am light engine off shed to Barrs Court. Shunts Barrs Court then works 1.14pm passenger service to Gloucester.
2b		1.10pm-2.40pm 1hr 30min	Shunting by engine off 8.15am Gloucester to Hereford freight.
2c		2.40pm-10.15pm 7hr 35min	Shunts Barrs Court Upside Yard [engine maybe off Pontrilas freight trip].
3	Worcester Sidings	Continuous	Shunts Worcester Sidings and works as required.
4	Show Yard	11am-6pm 7hr	Works 11am trip Worcester Sidings to Show Yard. Shunts Gas Works, then Painter Bros. Sidings at 2pm. Works trip to Worcester Sidings with London District traffic to connect 4.35pm Hereford to Gloucester freight. Works 5pm trip Show Yard to Worcester Sidings. Shunts Worcester Sidings Downside as required and thence to Barton.
5	Moorfields	7.30am-7.30pm 12hr	6.45am light engine off shed to Barrs Court. Works 7.30am trip to Moorfields, then shunts and works trips to Worcester Sidings. Shunts Worcester Downside 11am-1.45pm, including Cripple Sidings 12.30-1.30pm then light engine to Barton. Works 2.5pm trip Barton to Barrs Court, then 3.15pm trip Barrs Court to Moorfields. Shunts Moorfields and works 7pm trip to Worcester Sidings.
6	Barton	8am-8.30pm 12hr 30min	Shunts Barton and works as required.

3F 0-6-0PT No. 9717 on Barrs Court Downside shunting duties attached to an ex-GWR shunting truck, viewed from College Road Bridge with cattle pens in the background. More cattle pens were to be found in Worcester Down Sidings near to the cattle market. Livestock was still regularly being conveyed on market days and often on the 4.35pm Hereford-Gloucester freight. The scene is undated, but predates No. 9717's withdrawal in December 1962. JOHN GOSS

2F 0-6-0PT No. 1613 pauses whilst shunting the north end of Worcester Sidings on 3 August 1964; the wistful-looking fireman is Ken Pilliner. Curving away to the right is the former Brecon branch, by this date only open as far as Eardisley, whilst the former Midland Railway Moorfields engine shed, closed in 1924, still stands in the background. P.J. GARLAND/ KIDDERMINSTER RAILWAY MUSEUM

3F 0-6-0PT No. 3729 busy shunting fitted vans in a typical 1961 yard scene. The driver can be seen looking back and taking instructions from the shunter. No. 3729 had two spells at Hereford from October 1960 to June 1961 and December 1962 to March 1963 withdrawal. John Goss

2F 0-6-0PT No. 1657, on the Barton Sidings pilot turn, has crossed to the upside to make a shunt behind the signal box on the short No. 25 stop-block siding by the shed exit. Several staff members discuss what happens next, whilst another strides purposefully away. There are no clues as to date here, as No. 1657 was a long-term resident from new in January 1955 to withdrawal on Shed closure. JOHN GOSS

2F 0-6-0PT No. 1667, with a Worcester Sidings designated ex-GWR shunting truck, makes a head shunt alongside the Hereford avoiding line. Hereford's 1600s were real time servers, No. 1667 being typical, having arrived new in January 1955 and working here until withdrawal on Depot closure. F.K. DAVIES/GREAT WESTERN TRUST

Pontrilas Station, twelve miles down the main line and looking here towards South Wales, was the destination for a daily pannier tank-worked trip from Hereford. The passenger station is photographed within months of closure in June 1958. Once the junction for the Golden Valley line, a Royal Ordnance ammunition stores depot remained open just onto the branch, along with the station goods yard, both situated behind the photographer at the Hereford end of the Station. Michael Hale/Great Western Trust

Pontrilas Goods Yard in 1958 with Hereford's 2F 0-6-0PT No. 1662 making a shunt adjacent to the passenger station. The Golden Valley branch leading to the Royal Ordnance Depot can be seen in the background, with the trip and brake van in the rear standing on the branch connection. There seems to have been a reasonable amount of traffic on offer that day. Michael Hale/Great Western Trust

Hereford Station

As a teenager, I would spend some weekday and most Sunday afternoons at the Station, interspersed with a cycle ride to the Shed. There was a particular flurry of activity on Sunday afternoons, when the 12.40pm Cardiff-Manchester and 11.15am Manchester-Cardiff crossed at around 2.30pm and this was followed by the 8.45am Plymouth-Liverpool and 11am Liverpool-Plymouth similarly crossing at about 3pm. These four services would produce a quartet of Castle or County 4-6-0s from Cardiff, Bristol or Shrewsbury depots. All were booked a four to six minutes station call. We would watch transfixed as the time-honoured routine was played out of the fireman clambering onto the rear of the tender directing the water bag whilst the driver, as befitting his seniority, stood by the platform water

Hereford Station looking north with the route from South Wales running into the up main platform on the left and the down island platform to the right. The middle roads in between were used for stabling coaching stock in between duties and where Hereford's station pilot would usually be found. The short bay platform on the left was for pre-loading parcels vans; out of view at the north end was a bay platform, where Brecon branch services often started. The up and down goods lines are on the far right. Ayleston Hill Signal Box on the extreme right controlled movements into and out of the Station. R.G. Nelson/Terry Walsh collection

Looking north
from the Station, the main line swings right towards Barrs Court Junction where it meets the Hereford avoiding line, running left to right out of sight in front of the gas holder. Brecon Curve is on the left leading towards Hereford's other freight yards, the engine shed and the Brecon branch. Meanwhile, Gloucester's 4MT 2-6-0 No. 6330 brings the 4.30pm Hereford Worcester Sidings-Gloucester branch freight across the layout from the Brecon Curve and onto the down goods line on 27 June 1962. DEREK CROSS

column, cotton waste in hand, controlling the water flow. While this was going on, the fireman would slide down the tender and pull coal forward to make for easier firing later on. Then miraculously, as the allotted departure time approached, the water bag would be swung away and the crew clambered back on board just as shrill platform whistles were sounded. Invariably, on cue, the locomotive's safety valve would explode and our Castle or County 4-6-0 would make a measured firm-footed start away from the Station, for as we all knew, a Western engine never slipped.

By autumn 1963, this Sunday afternoon scene was more likely to produce a Hymek and two Warships, with only the slightly re-timed 11.5am Manchester-Cardiff still steam-hauled. All the more valued Cardiff East Dock Castles worked the latter, with No. 5091 *Cleeve Abbey* on the 27 October, and No. 5073 *Blenheim* on the 8 and 15 December 1963. If all went quiet around the Station, the simmering

Hereford Hall or Castle on station pilot duty would always be worthy of closer examination.

On weekdays, it would be of particular interest to see what Gloucester or Brecon had turned out on their services, whilst Worcester or Old Oak Common Castles would run in on those from Paddington. Though the majority of mainline freight trains ran via the Hereford avoiding line, a number were routed via the Station over the up and down goods lines which could produce a variety of engines from depots far and wide. Indeed, look at most photographed express-passenger departures towards Cardiff or the West of England, and a freight train will be seen in the background on the down goods patiently waiting a train path. Station visits always were about watching a continuing parade of services with the expectation of what the next whistle in the distance or signal coming off might bring.

Barrs Court Junction looking towards the Station with the signal box perched on top of the embankment. Looking from the north, the first four tracks swing around to the left towards the passenger Station, with the left hand pair the start of the goods lines running behind the station platforms. The freight-only Hereford avoiding line leaves to the right; the route taken by many through freight trains including those calling to work at Worcester Sidings. M. HALE/GREAT WESTERN TRUST

Hereford Station south end on a busy afternoon in the early 1960s, with Hereford's 5MT 4-6-0 No. 4990 *Clifton Hall* on Station Pilot duty whilst a 4MT 4300 2-6-0, waits departure with a Gloucester branch service. A Stanier 8F 48000 2-8-0 awaits the road, safety valve blowing high into the sky, on the down goods with a freight train for South Wales. Ayleston Hill Signal Box is on the right. JOHN GOSS

6MT 4-6-0 No. 1009 *County of Carmarthen* gently brings a Manchester/Liverpool to the West of England express into Hereford's down island platform on 1 June 1961 and will shortly come to a stand at the platform-end water column. Now a St Phillip's Marsh engine, it is still carrying its previous 82A Bristol Bath Road shed plate, despite that having closed for diesel depot conversion nine months earlier. JOHN GOSS

Castle 4-6-0 No. 5043 *Earl of Mount Edgcumbe*, of Old Oak Common on Hereford's middle road on 4 June 1960, having brought in a Paddington-Hereford service. After a short turnaround, it would work back as far as Worcester Shrub Hill with the next return service. There, a fresh Castle would set back the main portion onto the three-coaches Hereford portion. The engine released off the incoming Hereford portion would then take the next London service forward. F.K. Davies/Great Western Trust

7P 4-6-0 No. 5099 *Compton Castle*, of Cardiff Canton, looking in immaculate condition, prepares to depart Hereford on Saturday, 4 June 1960 with a South Wales-Manchester express. The signal box at the north end of the Station is in the background. F.K. Davies/Great Western Trust

5MT 4-6-0 No. 5904 *Kelham Hall*, of Bristol St Phillip's Marsh, is an unusual choice for Station Pilot on 1 November 1961. The Depot must have been short of home-based Halls and the Shed Foreman substituted a spare visiting engine. The eagle-eyed will have spotted the engine is coupled to the unique Collett eight-wheeled tender, No. 2586, built in 1931 and which was its regular partner. JOHN GOSS

5MT 4-6-0 No. 5952 *Cogan Hall*, on Station Pilot duty in the early 1960s. A Hereford regular, it arrived in August 1959 from Worcester, staying until replaced by the Castles at Hereford in November 1963. It then moved on to Cardiff East Dock. The engine is standing at the north end of the down island platform, having backed onto a set of stock which it will now propel out towards the carriage sidings. It was common practice, as shown here for the Hereford Station pilot to carry express-passenger head lamps. JOHN GOSS

7P 4-6-0 No. 7012 *Barry Castle* carrying a 1Z26 head code at Hereford with a terminated special passenger service in the early 1960s. During this period it was first allocated to Old Oak Common and then Wolverhampton Stafford Road, which narrows the service's origin to either London or the West Midlands. Castles were beautifully proportioned engines, particularly in their single-chimney form as seen here. JOHN GOSS

6MT 4-6-0 No. 1009 *County of Carmarthen* shunts a parcels van on or off the express-passenger train in the up main platform in around 1958. A Bristol Bath Road engine, the depot's Counties alternated with Castles on North & West express-passenger services. Both Bristol and Shrewsbury depots had sizeable County allocations at this time. M. HALE/GREAT WESTERN TRUST

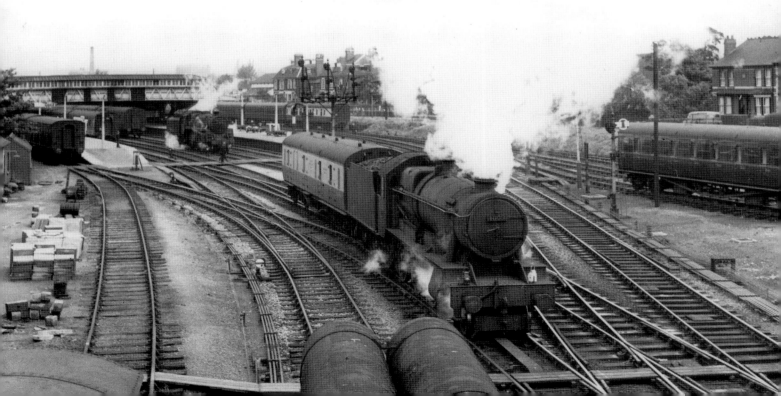

5MT 4-6-0 No. 6943 *Farnley Hall*, of Cardiff Canton in an atmospheric shot, with smoke swirling around the engine on a dark, wet miserable 1961 day. It is awaiting departure with a northbound service from Hereford whilst a set of Gloucester branch stock is stabled on the middle road. John Goss

7P 4-6-0 No. 7032 *Denbigh Castle* from Old Oak Common has recently terminated on a service from Paddington. It has been detached and has drawn forward to the platform-end signal to await clearance to proceed. The engine will then run back through the Station for turning before working back the next London service. John Goss

7P 4-6-0 No. 4079 *Pendennis Castle* of Bristol St Phillip's Marsh, taking water during its Hereford Station call whilst the driver briefly returns to the cab. The train is the 12.45pm Cardiff to Manchester on Boxing Day 1963, with a Sunday service in operation. The engine working that day is unusual, with a Bristol engine on what should be a Cardiff East Dock turn. Michael Jennings

7P 4-6-0 No. 4080 *Powderham Castle* from Cardiff East Dock, brings the 11.05am Manchester-Cardiff into Hereford on Sunday, 5 April 1964. It had been in store for six months the previous year and its cab side number plate is missing. Meanwhile, a Hymek diesel-hydraulic is about to pass with the 12.45pm Cardiff-Manchester, this train having succumbed to diesel haulage since the earlier 26 December 1963 photo. Michael Jennings

6P/5F Patriot 4-6-0 No. 45505 *The Royal Army Ordnance Corps,* safety valve blowing, is ready to depart Hereford with the 9.15am Manchester-Swansea on 4 July 1959. A Manchester Longsight engine, this was the only daytime LMR express-passenger turn south of Shrewsbury, working through to Pontypool Road and returning with an afternoon service. F.K. Davies/Great Western Trust

6P/5F Patriot 4-6-0 No. 45520 *Llandudno* heads out of Hereford with a thirteen-coach northbound express-passenger service in either 1959 or 1960. This lengthy train must be from the West Country, the LMR engine having taken over at Pontypool Road. Meanwhile, a Hereford 0-6-0PT, complete with ex-GWR shunting truck, is on the Barrs Court downside shunting turn. JOHN GOSS

7P Royal Scot 4-6-0 No. 46137 *The Prince of Wales's Volunteers (South Lancashire)* of Manchester Longsight depot runs into Hereford's down island platform with a southbound express from Manchester in 1960. Both driver and fireman are peering out of the locomotive cab and will shortly alight to go through the watering routine. JOHN GOSS

Worcester line, where they supported Worcester and Old Oak Common Castles during the continuing diesel traction shortfall.

Hereford's Castles had a single, but demanding North & West route express-passenger diagram of twenty-eight hours duration. This began at 2am each morning, taking over the 12.05am Cardiff-Liverpool and working it through to Shrewsbury. It then returned with the 9.30am Manchester-Cardiff, through to destination. After a short break on shed, it worked the 4.45pm Cardiff-Liverpool back to Shrewsbury. There it took another break before working home the 4.02am Shrewsbury-Hereford mail and news the next morning, arriving back at 5.50am. The locomotive was then cycled onto a later starting diagram, another Hereford Castle having restarted this turn at 2am that morning. Hereford Castles noted working the 9.30am Manchester-Cardiff included No. 7022 *Hereford Castle* on 20 November; No. 5055 *Earl of Eldon* on 23 November; No. 5000 *Launceston Castle* on 28 December 1963 and 1 January 1964 and No. 5055 *Earl of Eldon* on 22 February 1964.

It is likely that the central part of the diagram was discontinued some months before the Hereford Castle fleet's final demise. It was reported in late March 1964 that the 9.30am Manchester-Cardiff had recently become diagrammed for a Brush Type 4 diesel-electric; these being delivered to Cardiff Canton and Bristol Bath Road at the time in large numbers. However, No. 5055 *Earl of Eldon* was noted on shed at Shrewsbury on 7 May 1964 and in June they were still definitely working the 12.05am Cardiff-Liverpool from Hereford. A week's sightings revealed an alternate day pattern with No. 5042 *Winchester Castle* on Monday, 8 and Wednesday, 10 June; No. 5056 *Earl of Powis* on Tuesday, 9 and Thursday, 11 June; and No. 5000 *Launceston Castle* on

Friday, 12 June 1964. On the latter date, the engine next worked the Southall-Wrexham Parcels and Milk Empties from Shrewsbury. Earlier on 19 March 1964, No. 5055 *Earl of Eldon* headed the 5.10pm Shrewsbury-Wolverhampton local, whilst No. 5000 *Launceston Castle* was noted passing through Wrexham with a Shrewsbury-bound freight on 11 April 1964. These fill-in jobs from Shrewsbury would have appeared due to the under-utilised engine now laying over there spare until working the 4.02am Shrewsbury-Hereford Mail and News the next morning.

The Hereford Station Pilot and Standby Locomotive duties principally involved shunting coaching stock off terminating Paddington and Gloucester line services along with occasional parcels van attachments. On a Sunday, there was little to do for engine or crew except sit and wait for the occasional Paddington terminator or a main-line locomotive failure. I would spend many a Sunday afternoon on the station platform in company with the chosen simmering Castle pilot on the station middle road.

Hereford's position midway between main rail centres meant it was regularly the port in a storm that ailing locomotives would limp to seeking assistance. It was more precisely fifty-five miles north of Cardiff, seventy miles north of Bristol via the Severn Tunnel and fifty-one miles south of Shrewsbury. When steam locomotives failed, it was usual for the offender to be changed and then limp off to shed for attention, providing additional regular repair work for the shed fitters. However, with diesels it was more usual, with no diesel repair facilities locally, to isolate the offender, and the standby engine pilot the train forward to Bristol, Cardiff or Shrewsbury. Such occasions increased during the winter when diesel steam-heating boiler failures were a problem.

No. 5055 *Earl of Eldon* **and No. 5000** *Launceston Castle* between duties on shed at Hereford on Sunday, 26 April 1964. I remember well that first Sunday afternoon shed visit in November 1963 when there they were together, Hereford's four new and unexpected Castle 4-6-0s. Externally in poor condition they would never the less prove to be hard working engines. KIDDERMINSTER RAILWAY MUSEUM

Hereford's Castles performed some sterling rescue work during this time. No. 5000 *Launceston Castle* was noted on 9 January 1964 leaving Hereford piloting failed Warship D853 *Thruster* on the 9.5am Liverpool-Plymouth. No. 5055 *Earl of Eldon* passed Filton Junction north of Bristol on 24 April 1964, running approximately sixty minutes late piloting a Warship, also on the 9.5am Liverpool-Plymouth. Northbound services included No. 5000 *Launceston Castle*, seen on 5 June 1964, racing through Craven Arms hauling Warship D838 *Rapid* and the 8am Plymouth-Liverpool.

With only four locomotives for its three diagrams, it was essential that Hereford had their engines promptly returned from these unscheduled workings. No doubt the Shed Running Foreman impressed on crews to stay with their engine and bring it back at all costs. This happened surprisingly regularly and after No. 5055 *Earl of Eldon* had piloted a Warship into Bristol on 24 April 1964, it was seen on Station Pilot duty at Hereford again the next day.

There does seem to have been some bias in the engines chosen for station pilot duties. The turn was dominated by Nos. 5000 *Launceston Castle* and 5055 *Earl of Eldon*, along with No. 5042 *Winchester Castle* after its arrival in April 1964. By contrast No. 7022 *Hereford Castle* was rarely used, being more usually allocated to the more onerous Worcester or North & West diagrams. This, coupled with the fact that the latter was not stopped once for 'unclassified repairs', suggests *Hereford Castle* was regarded as the best performing Castle at Hereford.

HEREFORD STATION PILOTS/STANDBY LOCOMOTIVES
NOVEMBER 1963-JUNE 1964
The Hereford Castles Allocation Period

Date	Locomotive	Depot
Th. 07/11/63	5000 *Launceston Castle*	86C
Tu. 19/11/63	6800 *Arlington Grange*	86B
Sun. 08/12/63	5000 *Launceston Castle*	86C
Sun. 15/12/63	5000 *Launceston Castle*	86C
Fri 20/11/63	5055 *Earl of Eldon*	86C
Sat. 21/12/63	6904 *Charfield Hall*	2D
Sun. 22/12/63	5952 *Cogan Hall*	88L
Th. 26/12/63	6928 *Underley Hall*	86G
Fri. 27/12/63	5073 *Blenheim*	88L
Sat. 28/12/63	5998 *Trevor Hall*	86G
Th. 09/01/64	5000 *Launceston Castle* (1)	86C
Sun. 19/01/64	6876 *Kingsland Grange* (2)	86G
Sun. 26/01/64	5055 *Earl of Eldon*	86C
Sat. 01/02/64	5055 *Earl of Eldon*	86C
Sun. 09/02/64	6958 *Oxburgh Hall* (2)	86G
Sun. 16/02/64	5055 *Earl of Eldon*	86C
Th. 20/02/64	6875 *Hindford Grange* (2)	82B
Sat. 22/02/64	6875 *Hindford Grange* (2)	82B
Sun. 23/02/64	7011 *Banbury Castle* (2)	85A
Sun. 01/03/64	5000 *Launceston Castle*	86C
Th. 05/03/64	5055 *Earl of Eldon*	86C
Sun. 08/03/64	5055 *Earl of Eldon*	86C
Sun. 22/03/64	5055 *Earl of Eldon*	86C
Wed. 25/03/64	5054 *Earl of Ducie* (from 86C to 85A w/e 21/03/64)	85A
Sun. 29/03/64	5055 *Earl of Eldon*	86C
Sun. 05/04/64	5000 *Launceston Castle*	86C
Tu. 07/04/64	5000 *Launceston Castle*	86C
Th. 09/04/64	5000 *Launceston Castle*	86C
Sat. 18/04/64	5055 *Earl of Eldon*	86C
Sun. 19/04/64	5055 *Earl of Eldon*	86C
Wed. 22/04/64	5055 *Earl of Eldon* 6958 *Oxburgh Hall* (late evening)	86C 86G

HEREFORD STATION PILOTS/STANDBY LOCOMOTIVES
NOVEMBER 1963-JUNE 1964
The Hereford Castles Allocation Period

Date	Locomotive	Depot
Th. 23/04/64	5055 *Earl of Eldon*	86C
Fri. 24/04/64	5055 *Earl of Eldon* (3) 6965 *Thirlestaine Hall* (3)	86C 86B
Sat. 25/04/64	5055 *Earl of Eldon*	86C
Mon. 27/04/64	5055 *Earl of Eldon*	86C
Sun. 03/05/64	5000 *Launceston Castle*	86C
Th. 07/05/64	5976 *Ashwicke Hall*	86G
Sun. 10/05/64	5000 *Launceston Castle*	86C
Sat. 16/05/64	5055 *Earl of Eldon*	86C
Sun. 17/05/64	5042 *Winchester Castle*	86C
Wed. 20/05/64	5042 *Winchester Castle*	86C
Sun 24/05/64	6934 *Beachamwell Hall* (4)	6D
Tu. 26/05/64	6856 *Stowe Grange*	85A
Th. 28/05/64	5000 *Launceston Castle*	86C
Sat. 30/05/64	5000 *Launceston Castle*	86C
Fri 05/06/64	5000 *Launceston Castle* (5)	86C
Sun. 07/06/64	5055 *Earl of Eldon*	86C
Th 11/06/64	5000 *Launceston Castle*	86C
Fri. 12/06/64	5042 *Winchester Castle*	86C
Tu. 16/06/64	5055 *Earl of Eldon*	86C
Sat. 20/06/64	5042 *Winchester Castle* 5055 *Earl of Eldon*	86C 86C
Sun. 21/06/64	5055 *Earl of Eldon*	86C
Fri. 26/06/64	5055 *Earl of Eldon*	86C
Sat. 27/06/64	5042 *Winchester Castle*	86C
Mon. 29/06/64	5042 *Winchester Castle*	86C

Notes:

1. No. 5000 *Launceston Castle* assisted D853 forward from Hereford on the 9.5am Liverpool to Plymouth.

2. Spare visiting engines often borrowed whilst two out of four Hereford Castles 5000 & 5054 were stopped for unclassified repairs between 19/01-25/02/64.

3. No. 5055 *Earl of Eldon* reported at Bristol assisting a failed Warship on the 9.5am Liverpool to Plymouth. No. 5055 would have been the booked Hereford standby locomotive with No. 6965 *Thirlestaine Hall* (86B) provided later in the day as a short notice station pilot replacement.

4. No. 6934 *Beachamwell Hall* (6D) used to replace failed No 70028 *Royal Star* forward from Hereford on the 4.5pm Manchester to Bristol.

5. No. 5000 *Launceston Castle* used to assist D838 forward from Hereford on the 8am Plymouth to Liverpool.

The need to reinstate steam haulage on Hereford-Worcester-Paddington services had been the driving force behind the Hereford Castle allocation. The route had a two-hour service frequency with Hereford departures at 6.20am, 8am *The Cathedrals Express*, 10.5am, 12.5pm, 2.5pm, 4.5pm and 6.5pm. Services left Paddington at 9.15am, 11.15am, 1.15pm,

3.15pm, 5.15pm *The Cathedrals Express* and 7.15pm.

By this date all services were formed with modern BR Mark 1 coaching stock, most reducing to a three or four-coach portion beyond Worcester Shrub Hill-Hereford. The Worcester portion was detached rear on services from Paddington and attached front returning to Paddington; the latter a more complex operation. This led in the pre-diesel era to three-legged diagram workings, with Old Oak Common and Worcester Castles dominating the service. Old Oak Castles would work through from Paddington-Hereford, with the Worcester portion detached from the rear. On the return, the engine would only work as far as Worcester Shrub Hill, drawing to a stand on the rear section of its long up platform. The incoming engine would then be detached and released through the mid-platform crossover. The main Worcester portion, already standing at the forward end of the platform complete with train engine for Paddington, would set back onto the Hereford portion for departure. The released Old Oak Common Castle would generally be the train engine from Worcester for the next Paddington service two hours later. Worcester Castles worked a similar three-legged diagram. Hereford, in those pre-diesel days, only had a small involvement, with a Hall limited to a single diagram working several services only as far as Worcester.

When steam was reinstated, it might be presumed, given the decision to base Castles at Hereford, that the Depot would share the through workings to Paddington. However, on most services a practice of changing engines at Worcester in both directions was introduced, with the Hereford Castles working a single intensive diagram shuttling back and fore between Hereford and Worcester. It has proved difficult to reconstruct the precise

diagrams for this section and it is likely that their composition changed two or three times during the period. However, we know Hereford was given a single daily Castle diagram and that this varied over time between two and three round trips to Worcester.

By early November 1963, Hereford's No. 5055 *Earl of Eldon* and Worcester's 5MT 4-6-0 No. 6856 *Stowe Grange* were regular performers between Hereford and Worcester, with each undertaking three round trips per day. These workings involved around a sixty-minute turnaround at Worcester Shrub Hill, followed by another at Hereford. Engines had to be turned and watered during the limited layovers. At Hereford, the Castle on Station Pilot duty assisted by shunting stock between platforms whilst the train engine ran off to turn and water. At Worcester, the engines turned via the Rainbow Hill triangle. Precision working was required and these tight sequential journey legs were more like new-style intensive diesel operations.

It was noted in November 1963 that an Old Oak Castle was working the last 7.15pm Paddington service through to Hereford, returning to London the next morning. I saw Old Oak's No. 7035 *Ogmore Castle* on Shed at Hereford on Sunday, 17 November 1963, almost certainly off the last Saturday evening service.

I recorded many of these Hereford Castle workings. On 3 April 1964, No. 5000 *Launceston Castle* took the 6.5pm Hereford-Paddington as far as Worcester, returning after a bare one-hour turnaround with the 5.15pm Paddington-Hereford. Now a popular choice on the Worcester diagram, *Launceston Castle* worked the 12.5pm Hereford-Paddington on 23 April, then I travelled behind it on the 4.5pm Hereford-Paddington on 25 April. On the 29 April, *Launceston Castle* performed at least three round trips with the 6.20am, 12.5pm and 4.5pm Hereford-Paddington. With its small fleet, Hereford certainly played its part in keeping services running during the diesel shortage.

By spring 1964, Hymeks were being seen back on some Paddington services, and from early May 1964 all services between Worcester and Paddington were diagrammed to be diesel hauled. There was, however, still some planned steam haulage between Worcester and Hereford until the beginning of the 1964 summer timetable that June. Even then, occasional diesel shortfalls could result in steam substitution, although now Worcester had to cover, for Hereford's Castle era had come to an end.

HEREFORD CASTLES MAINTENANCE RECORDS

Engine	Built	Previous Scheduled Swindon Works	Unclassified Depot Repairs	Mileage as at 28/12/63
5000	1926	HG September 1961	Hereford 20/1-25/2/64	1,870,200
5054	1936	HG September 1962	Hereford 18/11-9/12/63 Hereford 19/1-13/3/64 Worcester 8/4-23/4/64*	1,412,394
5055	1936	HI February 1962	-	1,439,975
7022	1949	HI December 1961	Worcester 23/3-16/4/64*	733,069
5042	1935	HG June 1962	-	1,339,221
5056	1936	HI March 1962	Hereford 10/4-1/6/64	1,434,833

Notes:
HG: Heavy General overhaul, HI: Heavy Intermediate overhaul.
*: Shopped for assessment for the May 1964 High-Speed Castle Special.

The four Castles allocation needed to achieve 75 per cent availability to cover the three daily diagrams. Such a small group with no additional cover was nevertheless vulnerable. It only required one locomotive to be stopped and 100 per cent availability was demanded from the rest. Hereford was particularly vulnerable in that it had no other engines suitable to step up, with nothing else larger than 4MT 5101 2-6-2Ts or 3MT 2251 0-6-0s, neither suitable for main-line passenger work. When the Depot was short, the usual practice was for the Shed Running Foreman to borrow a spare visiting Hall off an unbalanced freight or with a lengthy scheduled layover. History does not record the extent to which this was to the detriment of their return workings.

On their arrival in autumn 1963, the Castles were, to put it mildly, somewhat care-worn and surviving photographs show most to be in poor external condition. Nos. 5000, 5055 and 7022 were all minus front number plates. No. 5055 was also missing a right-hand cab side number plate. All their name plates were thankfully firmly in place and remained so during their Hereford stay. Mechanically, they were mostly sound and there is no evidence of any failures in traffic, although locomotive record cards do show a succession of individual engines being stopped for 'unclassified repairs'. In January 1964, No. 5054 *Earl of Ducie* was out of traffic for seven weeks, probably partly waiting replacement parts. Most seriously, between 20 January and 25 February 1964, both No. 5000 *Launceston Castle* and No. 5054 *Earl of Ducie* were both stopped together, leaving only two Castles operational. This must have put the Depot under considerable pressure. Even so, at a time when work in excess of laid-down financial limits led to immediate withdrawal, none of Hereford's Castles met that fate.

No. 5054 *Earl of Ducie* was reported locally as being the last engine to have valves and pistons worked upon at Hereford. Despite its poor availability record, or perhaps because of the excellent work done by Hereford Shed staff to bring it up to standard, it was unexpectedly transferred to Worcester in March 1964. It received further attention there and became the star performer on the High-Speed Castle run of 9 May 1964. It worked the final leg from Bristol-Paddington when it achieved a top speed of 96mph. This was a clear indication that, given proper care and attention, Castles were still capable of delivering quality performances.

It would be inappropriate to leave the subject of Hereford maintenance and repair without reference to a visiting Castle that took up temporary, but long-term residence at the Depot. Cardiff East Dock's No. 5092 *Tresco Abbey* failed on 1 May 1963 whilst working the 12.05pm Manchester-Plymouth, limping on to Shed where I saw it in the repair shop the next day. Clearly it had suffered a catastrophic failure and was condemned at the end of July without returning to its home depot. Taking up residence outside the Shed, it became a permanent fixture for the next twelve months. Other locomotives were withdrawn and left for scrap, but not *Tresco Abbey*. I had previously thought that either the defect had rendered it immovable or that officialdom had somehow forgotten it, but a more plausible theory is that it was seen as a useful source of Castle spares for the Hereford fleet, given little would have been available by now from Swindon Works. Interestingly, it eventually left for a South Wales scrap yard in late July 1964, barely a month after the transfer away of Hereford's

Castles. Last seen at Hereford on 13 July, it had reached Pontypool Road on 19 July in the company of withdrawn County 4-6-0 No. 1005 *County of Devon* and 2251 0-6-0 No. 2241.

By June 1964, Brush Type 4 diesels had taken over almost all Warship, Hymek and residual steam diagrams on North & West express-passenger services. However, I was to discover that, in the middle of the night, Hereford's Castles, for a few weeks more, worked the 12.5am Cardiff-Liverpool between Hereford and Shrewsbury, returning with the next morning News and Mails from Shrewsbury. Meanwhile, Hymeks had returned in force on the Hereford-Paddington services and Hereford's Castle diagram to Worcester was no more. In theory, the necessity for a Station Pilot/Standby Locomotive remained, but the decision was taken that it could no longer be justified and the station pilot requirement was downgraded to a shunting engine turn.

Nos. 5000 *Launceston Castle* and 5056 *Earl of Powis* were last seen by me on shed on Wednesday, 17 June, officially transferring to Oxley that week ending. *Earl of Powis* was seen passing through Kidderminster light engine en route for Oxley on its transfer move that Saturday, 20 June 1964. The two arrived in time to become part of an enlarged fleet of ten Castles at Oxley for summer Saturday holiday trains from Wolverhampton Low Level to the South Coast, as far as Oxford or Kensington Olympia, and to the West of England, via Stratford-upon-Avon as far as Bristol. Both ex-Hereford engines worked tirelessly throughout the summer and typically, on Saturday, 1 August, at least six Oxley Castles were present in the Bristol area off these services.

The pair's departure to Oxley left just two Castles at Hereford for a further week. My lasting memory of these noble steeds was on Saturday, 20 June

1964. Then Nos. 5042 *Winchester Castle* and 5055 *Earl of Eldon* were together on Main Line Standby / Station Pilot duty, it being traditional practice to turn out two standbys on summer Saturdays. One was standing in the station middle road chimney facing northbound whilst the other was chimney facing southbound. They were ready for any final call to arms as a continuous parade of West Country holiday expresses passed through that Saturday. Both were reallocated to Gloucester Horton Road a week later. *Winchester Castle* was last seen by me on Station Pilot duty on Monday, 29 June and *Earl of Eldon* on shed the following day. They travelled under their own steam over the Hereford-Gloucester branch to their new home, finally bringing to an end Hereford's Castle Indian Summer. Several weeks later, on Saturday, 11 July 1964, the Station Pilot was Hereford's 0-6-0PT No. 4623; it just wasn't quite the same.

Taking a measured look back on those distant times, Hereford's Castles made an important and largely reliable contribution to the area's main-line operations during what was a difficult dieselisation transition period. Sometimes under repair, they were reliable when working, all the more remarkable given that Castle scheduled works overhauls had ceased the previous year and most were high-mileage engines. These relatively complex locomotives must have presented a significant challenge to Hereford's maintenance staff and it is to their credit that a respectable performance was maintained to the end.

No. 5000 *Launceston Castle* pulls away from Shrewsbury having just taken over the 9.30am Manchester-Cardiff from an LMR engine on 1 January 1964. This was the second leg of a demanding twenty-eight-hours diagram on North & West line passenger work. R.G. NELSON/TERRY WALSH COLLECTION

No. 5000 *Launceston Castle* is back on shed at Hereford the following morning, having completed the arduous North & West route passenger diagram at 5.50am, when it brought the newspaper train from Shrewsbury into Hereford. R.G. Nelson/Terry Walsh collection

No. 5054 *Earl of Ducie*, having recently been transferred from Llanelly, clearly has problems, standing on No. 5 road at the back of the Shed on 20 November 1963. It would be stopped for 'unclassified repairs' until 9 December, and again early the following year when valves and pistons were worked upon. R.G. Nelson/Terry Walsh collection

No. 5055 *Earl of Eldon* has just taken over the 11.15am Paddington-Hereford at Worcester Shrub Hill on 13 November 1963, soon after arrival at Hereford. It was immediately pressed into service alongside Worcester and Old Oak Common Castles to release Hymek diesel-hydraulics to assist with diesel locomotive shortages elsewhere on the Western Region. R.G. NELSON/TERRY WALSH COLLECTION

No. 5055 *Earl of Eldon* is on Hereford Station Pilot and main-line locomotive standby duty on 16 May 1964. Its principal task was shunting empty stock off terminating services, unless an express-passenger train locomotive failure occurred. Meanwhile Gloucester's 4MT 2-6-0 No. 6349 has just arrived with a branch passenger service from Gloucester. MICHAEL JENNINGS

No. 5042 *Winchester Castle* on Station Pilot duty the following day, 17 May 1964, standing on the goods lines behind the Station. It at least boasted a full set of number and name plates, although its front chimney lip had a nasty dent caused by an unexplained impact. No. 5042 arrived from Cardiff East Dock in April 1964 to replace one of the transfers to Worcester. MICHAEL JENNINGS

No. 5056 *Earl of Powis* had also arrived as a replacement from Cardiff East Dock in April 1964, shown here on Shed at Hereford on 10 April 1964. It had been failed on arrival for 'unclassified repairs' and fire bricks piled high on the footplate tell a story. One can imagine the air was blue as the Shed Foreman marched up to the Shed Master's office to report they had been sold a pup. JOHN HODGE

No. 5056 *Earl of Powis* on 27 April 1964, having been moved into the repair shops, where work was being carried out. They must have done a good job, as when the engine left Hereford for Oxley in June 1964, it spent a successful summer working Wolverhampton to West of England holiday expresses. R.G. NELSON/TERRY WALSH COLLECTION

No. 5092 *Tesco Abbey*, a Cardiff East Dock Castle, had suffered a catastrophic failure at Hereford working the 12.05pm Manchester-Plymouth on 1 May 1963. It was subsequently withdrawn without returning to its home depot. For some unexplained reason, it languished at Hereford for fourteen months until late July 1964, when it eventually left for scrap. It may well have provided useful spares for the Hereford Castle fleet and is pictured here on 13 February 1964. R.G. NELSON/TERRY WALSH COLLECTION

No. 7022 *Hereford Castle*, having terminated with the Hereford portion of the 9.15am from Paddington on 22 April 1964. Transferred to Worcester two weeks earlier, it continued to be a regular visitor to Hereford on these services. The best of the Hereford Castles, it had spent much of its time on main-line passenger work and rarely on the less onerous station pilot duty. R.G. NELSON/TERRY WALSH COLLECTION

No. 5055 *Earl of Eldon* on station pilot duty at Hereford on Saturday, 16 May 1964. The platform signal at the rear of the train is off and the engine is propelling the empty stock from a terminated Paddington service out of the Station towards the carriage sidings. JOHN HODGE

No. 5055 *Earl of Eldon* returned into the Station a short while later with the same stock for the next Paddington service. The eagle-eyed will spot that since the previous photograph, the formation has been reduced from four to three coaches. It was standard practice for Hereford's station pilot to carry express-passenger head lamps and this was not an indicator that it would work the train forward. JOHN HODGE

No. 5054 *Earl of Ducie*, now a Worcester engine, leaves Hereford towards Newport with an Oxford University Railway Society Special from Paddington on Saturday, 16 May 1964. Now a much sought after engine for specials and in pristine condition, it had achieved 96mph on the high-speed Plymouth-Paddington special the previous Saturday. Meanwhile, Pontypool Road's No. 6850 *Cleeve Grange* waits patiently to follow with a South Wales-bound freight train. John Hodge

No. 5054 *Earl of Ducie*, having just left Hereford Station, accelerates away towards Newport with the same train on 16 May 1964. The engine had come a long way since being failed in filthy condition on arrival at Hereford from storage at Llanelly the previous November. Michael Jennings

No. 5000 *Launceston Castle* hurries failed Warship diesel-hydraulic No. D838 *Rapid* through Craven Arms at speed on the 8am Plymouth-Liverpool on 5 June 1964. No. 5000 had been on station pilot duty at Hereford when called upon to provide assistance forward. Just two weeks later, its and the other Castles' duties at Hereford would be discontinued. No. 5000 would accompany No. 5056 *Earl of Powis* to Oxley where they would perform sterling work on summer Saturday holiday expresses from Wolverhampton to the West Country. DEREK CROSS

8F 2-8-0 No. 3828, of Croes Newydd, pulls away from Barton on the Hereford avoiding line in 1960 with a down freight from Chester's Saltney Yard for South Wales. JOHN GOSS

8F 2-8-0 No. 3830, of Newport Ebbw Junction, heads a northbound freight of small coal, probably from Rogerstone Yard in Newport's Western Valley, under the Aylestone Hill road bridge past Hereford Station on 11 June 1964. The furthest signal has been cleared to bring the train across the layout and onto the Up Goods around the back of the Station. DEREK CROSS

8F 2-8-0 No. 3830, of Newport Ebbw Junction takes the Up Goods around the Station on 11 June 1964 with a freight train from South Wales. Meanwhile Llanelly's Stanier 8F 2-8-0 No. 48409 stands on the Down Goods, awaiting a train path with a freight train for Llandilo Junction. On station pilot duty in the distance is Hereford's Castle 4-6-0 No. 5055 *Earl of Eldon*. DEREK CROSS

Ledbury Sub-shed and Banking Duties

Ledbury is situated thirteen miles east of Hereford on the main line to Worcester, the West Midlands and London. The Station was the first principal calling point after leaving Hereford, with a regular passenger service to Worcester and onwards to either Paddington via Oxford or Birmingham Snow Hill. Ledbury had also once been the end of a branch line from Gloucester from where both passenger and freight services were withdrawn in July 1959. After this, a truncated branch freight trip continued to run from Gloucester as far as Dymock. The main line though Ledbury was also an important long-distance freight route from South Wales to the West Midlands, with a lesser number heading for the Oxford area. Additionally, a daily freight trip ran from Worcester to Hereford and back serving local stations, which was worked by a Worcester engine.

Immediately beyond Ledbury Station is the single-bore Ledbury Tunnel, followed closely by Colwall Tunnel, both burrowing through the steeply-rising Malvern Hills. Initially trains encountered a tough two-mile climb out of Ledbury at 1 in 70/80, this section including the sulphurous single-bore Ledbury Tunnel. Beyond there, the gradient eased slightly, but remained challenging as far as the summit at Colwall, five miles from its start point. All freight trains, except the Hereford-Worcester freight trip, were booked to receive banking assistance. The powerful exhaust from hard-working engines would hit the narrow single-bore tunnel roof and swirl downwards, enveloping all that lay around. Several firemen who had worked both long-distance freight and banking duties when on loan to Ledbury, described tying wet handkerchiefs over their faces and sitting on the cab floor barely able to see the driver on the other side of the cab. A little unusually compared with other inclines, banking engines here worked smokebox trailing up the gradient and through the tunnel in an attempt to mitigate the effect of the exhaust fumes on the banking crew.

Located behind Ledbury's up Station platform was the bank engine stabling siding, the site technically described as a sub-shed although there was no actual building. In addition to the facilities described in the shed plan caption, behind and to the left-hand side of the coaling platform was a small corrugated iron store or lamp hut. Beyond it was a flat-roofed brick-built train crew mess

LEDBURY SHED

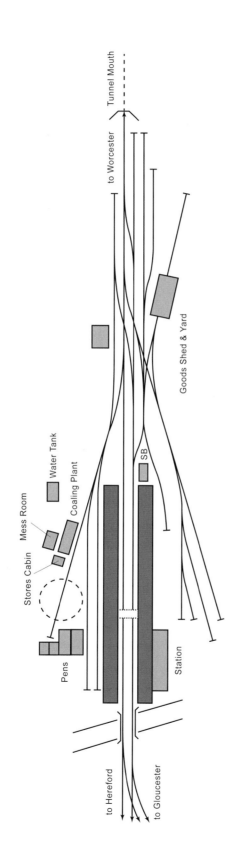

Ledbury Shed was located behind the up Station platform. There was no shed building, just a bank engine stabling siding with a short coaling platform edged with a rather fragile-looking corrugated iron veranda which gave footplate crews limited protection from the weather. The stabling siding led to a small little-used turntable, added in 1885. There were two further short sidings between the coaling stage and the station platform, one of which often contained wagons of locomotive coal.
BY RICHARD SODDY

room with a thin stove-pipe chimney protruded from the roof. A water tank was located on higher ground to the rear of the coaling plant with gravity-fed water columns located on both up and down Station platform ends.

Ledbury had been a Hereford Sub-shed since GWR days with, from the mid-1950s, a single Collett 5205 8F 2-8-0T out-based there. A spare engine of the same class was kept at Hereford. In January 1958, the allocation comprised Nos. 5226 and 5243, to which No. 5245 was added in November 1958. It is not easy to explain this later over provision as, by this date, Hereford had been taken out of long-distance freight work, which might have provided an additional duty. Nos. 5245 and 5226 were transferred away in August and September 1959 respectively, leaving No. 5243 on its own. It was nominally transferred to Worcester in February 1960, coincidental with the main shed responsibility for Ledbury changing from Hereford to Worcester. This was at the time that Hereford itself changed from a Worcester to a Newport District motive power depot. This change is sometimes incorrectly reported as happening in January 1961, but that was the date that the official BR shed coding book supplement was issued, changing Hereford's shed code from 85C to 86C. The actual responsibility transfer had occurred earlier, in February 1960.

The banking engine was on duty continuously from 6am Monday morning

Ledbury bank engine stabling siding, which was designated a sub-shed, there being the essential elements of a coaling facility, a small train crew depot and a single banking engine which was out-based here all week. On Saturday 19 September 1959, we find Hereford's Collett 5205 8F 2-8-0T No. 5243 awaiting banking duties. In the foreground, modellers will notice an ex-GWR gas lamp standard which will have been replaced by electric lighting in a later photo. R.G. NELSON/TERRY WALSH COLLECTION

until after the last freight train had passed in the early hours of Sunday morning. The latter time could vary, but in the winter 1960/61 timetable this was the 11.45pm (Sat) Cardiff-Oxley Sidings, booked to stop for a banking engine at 4.40am. No doubt an anxious crew, wanting to get home to their beds, would contact the Ledbury signalman for any news of what may have been a doubtfully punctual service. The banker then ran light engine to Hereford Shed for its day of rest and possible exchange with a shed mate for the following week. It was booked from Hereford back to

Ledbury for a 6am Monday morning start. After responsibility transferred to Worcester, the light engine movement would be to and from there, the winter 1960/61 working timetable showing a 5.15am Mondays Only light engine from Worcester Shed to Ledbury. An official September 1961 footplate staff return shows there were three drivers and three firemen (one a vacancy) based here. This would have been the absolute minimum staffing to cover the three shifts spread over a twenty-four-hour period, and relief for rest days, sickness and holidays would have had to come from the main

Journey's end and the 12.42hrs from Hereford has terminated at Three Cocks Junction on 10 October 1962. There is time for the crew to chat as the tail lamp is brought from the back of the train, as 2MT 2-6-0 No. 46503 prepares to run around. It will form the 2.15pm back to Hereford. Passengers here have a seven-minute connection into the 12.30pm Builth Road to Brecon whilst, the return service to Hereford will have a similar good connection from Brecon. RON HERBERT

Three Cocks Junction Station sign boasting a wide range of connectional possibilities, although in reality the routes from both Hereford and Moat Lane Junction were heavy loss makers. The advertised connection for Llandrindod Wells will be via a further change at Builth Road and to the Cambrian Coast at Moat Lane Junction. M. Hale/Great Western Trust

The ICI Chemicals train, the 12.05pm Hereford Barrs Court-Dowlais via Three Cocks and Talyllyn Junctions, prepares to depart on 12 March 1960. The train is headed by Hereford 3F 0-6-0PTs Nos. 8722 and 3728. Both are worked by Hereford footplate crews throughout for this tough trip over the wild and windswept Brecon Beacons. Michael Bland/Transport Treasury

Hay-on-Wye in an atmospheric scene as the 12.05pm Hereford-Dowlais ICI tank train pauses to take water on a filthy wet 12 March 1960. The train is headed by a pair of Hereford 3F 0-6-0PTs, Nos. 8722 and 3728. MICHAEL BLAND/TRANSPORT TREASURY

A breather at Talgarth between Three Cocks and Talyllyn Junctions. Hereford's 3F 0-6-0PTs Nos. 8722 and 3728 with the 12.05pm Hereford-Dowlais ICI tanks train on 12 March 1960. No. 8722 entered traffic in April 1931, arriving at Hereford from Worcester in August 1958 and moving on to Cardiff Canton in July 1960. No. 3728 entered service in July 1937. A Hereford time server arriving in March 1938, it only moved on to Radyr in October 1964, coincidental with Hereford's shed closure. MICHAEL BLAND/TRANSPORT TREASURY

Self-help banking duties. The 12.05pm Hereford-Dowlais ICI tanks train on 12 March 1960 has reached Talybont, the start of the challenging 1 in 38 'seven miles bank' to Torpantau. No. 8722 has run around to the rear and, after taking water, will bank its own train to the summit. Further ahead is the single-bore Beacon Tunnel and beyond that the wild and wind swept Torpantau station. MICHAEL BLAND/TRANSPORT TREASURY

Torpantau Station. In this undated view, only the leading engine of the 12.05pm Hereford-Dowlais ICI tanks train, Hereford's 3F 0-6-0PT No. 9665, is in view. The signalman on the ground is about to exchange single line tokens with the fireman. The weather conditions were so bleak here that the signal box side wall has been faced with slates for additional protection against the driving rain. Just after passenger service withdrawal, the freight service was suspended for a time due to 'icicles in the tunnel', a rather unique delay cause. M. HALE/GREAT WESTERN TRUST

The Brecon branch freight trip shunts traffic at Eardisley, which, since passenger service withdrawal, has become the limit of train operations. Its 19 August 1964 and Hereford's 3MT 0-6-0 No.2242 is berthing wagons under the direction of the guard, shunting pole in hand. We also get a fascinating elevated view of the cab interior, driver on the regulator easing the engine forward, whilst the firemen feeds coal into the bright and glowing firebox. Ben Ashworth

The return freight trip, headed by 3MT 0-6-0 No. 2242, is ready to leave Eardisley for Hereford. on 19 August 1964. The leading mineral wagon, with fuel for Credenhill's RAF Camp's boilers, will be put off there on the way back. The former route leaving to the left is the ex-GWR branch line to Titley Junction and Kington. Eardisley Signal Box is of Midland Railway design dating from 1893. BEN ASHWORTH

Hereford to Gloucester Branch – Operational Duties

The Hereford-Gloucester route was a delightful ex-GWR branch line engineered to the broad gauge and running through undulating rural countryside. The principal intermediate station was Ross-on-Wye, junction for the former Wye Valley branch line to Monmouth. It was a busy market town with a population of around 10,000 and the historic access point for the Wye Valley tourist area. What also made the Hereford-Gloucester branch line a little different was the fact that, instead of running to a country terminus, it linked two main centres on the rail network.

Services left Hereford in a south-easterly direction, travelling for the first mile towards South Wales before branching off at Rotherwas Junction. The Gloucester branch had in fact been the original route out of the Station, opening in 1855 and pre-dating what became known as the Hereford Curve, which opened in 1866 between Rotherwas and Red Hill Junctions, where it joined the original route to South Wales via the now freight-only Hereford avoiding line.

At Rotherwas Junction, there was a rail-served ordinance depot that had seen peak activity in the First and Second World Wars, but by the 1960s was working on a much reduced scale. The branch line's next twenty-one miles was single track with passing places as far as Grange Court Junction, where the main line into Gloucester was joined. Maximum branch line speed was a surprisingly low 35mph and most passenger services called at all stations.

Hereford Station in 1958, with Hereford's remarkably clean 4MT 2-6-2T No. 4115 picking up a set of coaching stock from the Station middle road to form the next Gloucester departure. J. Goss

Dinedore Tunnel is approached by Hereford's 4MT 2-6-2T No. 4115 and Gloucester's 4MT 2-6-0 No. 6330 double-heading the 4.04pm Gloucester-Hereford in July 1961. No. 4115 is the booked train engine and No. 6330 is hitching a lift to Hereford to work back with the unbalanced 7.35pm Hereford-Gloucester freight. John Goss

Hereford Station and journey's end is approached by Hereford's 4MT 2-6-2T No. 4135 with a Gloucester to Hereford service on 27 June 1962. The signal is off for the up main platform, and the carriage and DMU stabling sidings can be seen coming in from the right. The 20mph speed-restriction board is a reminder of the maximum permitted speed throughout the Barrs Court area on all running lines. Derek Cross

Hereford Station with a terminated Gloucester to Hereford service on 25 July 1964, headed by Hereford's 4MT 2-6-2T No. 4161. A staff member is placing a tail lamp on the front coach and the stock will shortly be shunted out of the platform onto the middle road by the station pilot coming on the other end of the train. Ayleston Hill Signal Box can be seen in the distance controlling the far end of the Station. MICHAEL JENNINGS

Branch freight trains could take between three to five hours for the complete journey between Hereford and Gloucester, waiting paths intermediately over the single line and, more importantly, shunting smaller stations along the way. In the late 1950s, there were three freight trains each way per day, a surprisingly high number for a rural branch line, although reductions occurred over the next few years. In addition to local traffic, some longer-distance traffic was conveyed, including London area traffic from Hereford on the 4.30pm Hereford Worcester Sidings to Gloucester, where it connected onwards for London. This service's load on Hereford market days was further swollen by a dozen or more cattle wagons, formed immediately behind the engine conveying a noisy cargo of livestock. The train was booked to stand on the Down Goods at Hereford Station from 4.37 to 5.20pm, waiting its booked path onto the single line. On market days, the noise emanating from the front portion of the train is well remembered echoing loudly across the Station.

Looking more closely at the freight train workings, the summer 1958 timetable comprised 8am, 4.35pm and 7.35pm departures from Hereford to Gloucester, and 5.10am, 8.15am and 6.40pm departures from Gloucester to

Hereford. Hereford had one branch freight locomotive diagram with a 3MT 2251 0-6-0 working the 8am Hereford and returning with the evening 6.40pm from Gloucester. Gloucester's 4MT 4300 2-6-0s were responsible for working the remaining trains. However, from the summer 1961 timetable, the 8.15am from Gloucester was withdrawn, and two of the Gloucester locomotive diagrams became passenger in one direction and freight in the other. These revised arrangements then applied up to branch closure. The first worked the 5.10am Gloucester to Hereford freight, then taking a lengthy break on shed before working the 2.43pm passenger train to Gloucester. The second Gloucester 4300 worked the 2.30pm Gloucester to Hereford passenger train arriving at 3.46pm. It then rapidly departed light engine for Worcester Sidings to work the 4.30pm freight back to Gloucester.

The final freight train of the day, the 7.35pm Hereford Barrs Court-Gloucester, became an unbalanced Gloucester turn after the withdrawal of the 8.15am Gloucester in the summer 1961 timetable. The booked light engine from Gloucester for this service often ran coupled inside the scheduled Hereford locomotive on the 4pm Gloucester-Hereford passenger service. In the final summer 1964 timetable and possibly earlier, the Gloucester engine was booked as a 3.35pm light engine from Gloucester to Hereford, although one wonders if to save single-line occupation the previous arrangements sometimes applied. This working was usually covered by a 4MT 4300 2-6-0, although by the summer 1964 timetable it was booked for a Gloucester 3F 5700 0-6-0PT.

A further change to the branch freight train arrangements occurred around October 1963. The 8.25am Hereford-Gloucester, worked by a Hereford 3MT 2251 0-6-0, was then altered to terminate at Grange Court Junction and return engine and van to Ross-on-Wye. There it formed the Lydbrook (former Monmouth) branch trip for the rest of the day. Ross-on-Wye Shed had closed in October 1963 and its dedicated Lydbrook branch trip engine discontinued. The Hereford engine then returned home after completing the Lydbrook trip as an additional 6.55pm Ross-on-Wye-Hereford freight. The previous return working of the 8.25am Hereford-Gloucester, the 6.35pm Gloucester-Hereford, was also discontinued from the same date. Local freight facilities had been withdrawn from intermediate branch stations at Holme Lacey, Ballingham, Fawley, Backney, Mitcheldean Road, Longhope and Grange Court from 12 August 1963, leaving only Ross-on-Wye and Lydbrook still handling goods traffic. The two Gloucester Churchward 4300 2-6-0 mixed passenger/freight locomotive diagrams were unaffected by these changes and continued to operate until branch closure.

Hereford to Gloucester – Saturdays Excepted
Passenger & Freight Locomotive Diagrams
15 June to 31 October 1964 Service Withdrawal
(Similar locomotive balances applied on Saturdays and on previous years)

Hereford 1: (SX) 41XX

Hereford		0655 Passenger
Gloucester	0802	0948 Passenger
Hereford	1104	1340 Passenger
Gloucester	1449	1600 Passenger
Hereford	1730	1802 Passenger
Gloucester	1915	2140 Passenger
Hereford	2247	

Hereford 2: (SX) 41XX

Hereford		0730 Passenger
Gloucester	0846	1215 Passenger
Hereford	1329	1630 Passenger
Gloucester	1747	1915 Passenger
Hereford	2021	

Hereford 3: (SX) 22XX (until Oct. 1963)

Hereford		0825 Freight
Gloucester	13XX	1835 Freight
Hereford	2320	

Applied until October 1963 when Ross Engine Shed closed (since 1960 a sub-shed of Gloucester) and revised working from October 1963 applied.

Hereford 3: (SX) 22XX (from Oct.1963)

Hereford		0825 Freight
Grange Court	1057	12/05 Engine & Van
Ross-on-Wye	12/45	1345 Freight (&)
Lydbrook	1405(&)	1725 Freight
Ross-on-Wye	1747	1855 Freight
Hereford	1940	

(&) Runs 20 mins later Thursdays only.
Hereford drivers & firemen: 0825 to Ross and 1855 Ross to Hereford.
Ross driver & fireman: 0958 from Ross (relieve 0825 freight) until 1747 arrive Ross.

Gloucester 1: (SX) 43XX*

Gloucester		0700 Passenger
Hereford	0830	1025 Passenger
Gloucester	1133	1425 Passenger
Hereford	1539	1630 Freight
Gloucester	2019	

Gloucester 2: (SX) 43XX*

Gloucester		0500 Freight
Hereford	1010	1438 Passenger
Gloucester	1553	1755 Passenger
Hereford	1909	2115 Passenger
Gloucester	2227	

*During 1964 2 x Gloucester 43XX diagrams became 1 x 43XX & 1 x Manor diagram.

Gloucester 3: 57XX

Gloucester		15/35 Light engine
Hereford	17/45	1840 Freight
Gloucester	2252	

The 8.25am Hereford to Grange Court Junction freight runs into Mitcheldean Road on 7 August 1964, watched by the signalman on the platform. The engine is Hereford's 3MT 0-6-0 No. 2242 and after terminating at Grange Court, it would return engine and van to Ross-on-Wye to work the Lydbrook branch freight trip. These revised arrangements had applied since the closure of the Ross-on-Wye sub-shed the previous October. BEN ASHWORTH

The 4.30pm Hereford-Gloucester Freight approaches Holme Lacey in July 1962, headed by Gloucester's 4MT 2-6-0 No. 6304. As well as branch traffic, this afternoon departure carried London traffic from Hereford for onward connection at Gloucester. JOHN GOSS

The 5am Gloucester-Hereford Freight approaches Fawley on an atmospheric cold autumn morning with mist rising from the surrounding fields. You can almost hear the silence being broken as the distant sound of a hard-working engine is heard getting louder. It is Saturday, 17 October 1964 and Gloucester's 4MT 2-6-0 No. 7320 is in charge. JOHN GOSS

The 5am Gloucester-Hereford Freight has now rounded the bend and is in full view. A light load is being conveyed consisting of some agricultural machinery, four grain wagons for a Hereford private siding, and a flat. Further traffic will undoubtedly have already been detached at the previous calling point, Ross-on-Wye. An ex-GWR brake van completes the scene. Just two weeks later and all of this will be history. JOHN GOSS

Time for a break. Gloucester's 3F 0-6-0PT No. 4698 and Hereford's No. 4623 pause for the crews to take a joint break at Grange Court Junction on 26 October 1964. No. 4623 has just terminated with the 8.25am freight from Hereford, and will shortly return engine and van to Ross-on-Wye to work the Lydbrook branch freight trip. No. 4698 has been on similar duties, having worked down the main line from Gloucester. BEN ASHWORTH

For many years on winter Sundays, when the Severn Tunnel was closed for planned engineering work, Manchester/Liverpool-Plymouth expresses were diverted from Hereford via Gloucester to Bristol Temple Meads, where the scheduled route was re-joined. From 27 October to 15 December 1957 and 5 January to 30 March 1958, the overnight 11.50pm (Sat) Manchester to Plymouth, 10.35 (Sun) Liverpool to Plymouth and 8.45am (Sun) Plymouth to Liverpool were diverted over the Hereford to Gloucester line. In subsequent years, the 11.50pm (Sat) Manchester Sleeping Car service was diverted even more imaginatively from Crewe via Wolverhampton (Low Level), the Dudley branch, Stourbridge Junction, Worcester and Gloucester to Bristol. However, the Hereford to Gloucester diversion of the Sunday

daytime services continued right up until line closure. The two daytime services crossed at Hereford with the 8.45am Plymouth to Liverpool, calling between 2.57-3.02pm, and the 11am Liverpool to Plymouth between 2.45-2.55pm. A little surprisingly, the advertised journey times between Hereford and Bristol were the same via the Severn Tunnel or the Gloucester diversion.

The locomotive arrangements for these diversions changed significantly over time. Historically, the heavier locomotives' restriction to 20mph over the branch effectively discounted them from practical use. Engine changes took place at Hereford in either direction with services over the branch usually in the hands of a pair of Churchward 4300 2-6-0s. The 8.45am Plymouth to Liverpool was usually worked by a pair of St Phillip's Marsh 4MT 4300 2-6-0s all the way from Bristol, although it is likely Gloucester footplate crews had worked the train forward from Gloucester.

In the early 1960s, the 'Red' category restriction was lifted and large engines, usually in the form of 7P Castle or 6MT County 4-6-0s, worked these trains through from Bristol to Shrewsbury. Less usual motive power was Shrewsbury-allocated ex-LMS 6P/5F Jubilee 4-6-0 No. 45577 *Bengal* on the 11am Liverpool to Plymouth on Sunday, 20 January 1963. On this Sunday, the line was also blocked between Hereford and Abergavenny, and the 10am Crewe-Newport parcels was also diverted over the branch worked by St. Phillip's Marsh 6MT County 4-6-0 No. 1020 *County of Monmouth*.

When Type 4 diesel-hydraulic Warships took over the West of England express passenger services during 1962, they too, from that winter, worked through over the Gloucester branch. On Sunday, 25 November 1962, the 8.45am Plymouth-Liverpool was noted headed by Plymouth Laira's Warship diesel-hydraulic No. D855 *Triumph*.

Throughout the period covered here, one or two long-distance parcels trains were also booked over the route on a daily basis. In the summer 1958 timetable, these comprised a 2am (MSX) Stockport to Bristol Parcels which passed Rotherwas Junction at 8.41am and a 6.30pm (FSX) Crewe to Bristol Parcels which left Hereford at 10.50pm and required intermediate branch signal boxes to stay open until its passage. Isolated parcels services continued to be similarly scheduled in subsequent years.

Main-line diversions took place on winter Sundays when the Severn Tunnel was closed for maintenance. One Sunday in 1960, we see the 8.40am Plymouth to Liverpool running into Hereford having been diverted from Bristol via Gloucester and Ross-on-Wye. It is no surprise to find a pair of Churchward 4MT 2-6-0s on the train; however it is interesting to note that both Nos. 6319 and 7301 are Bristol St Phillip's Marsh engines and have worked through from Bristol. In the background, Gloucester's No. 7312 and another class member out of shot wait to back onto the similarly-diverted 10.30am Liverpool to Plymouth. JOHN GOSS

Main-line diversion. Bristol St Phillip's Marsh's 4MT 2-6-0s Nos. 7332 and 6378 burst out of Lea Tunnel with the diverted 8.40am Plymouth to Liverpool on Sunday, 11 March 1962. These trains were an unexpected winter Sunday bonus over this fascinating branch line. Ben Ashworth

Main-line diversion. Severn Tunnel Junction's 4MT 2-6-0 No. 7328, carrying express passenger train head lamps and driven by Hereford's John Hick, has backed up to Llanelly's No. 6310 in the middle road at the Station. It is a 1960 Sunday and they are preparing to take over the 10.30am Liverpool-Plymouth diverted via Ross-on-Wye and Gloucester. The engine sourcing from these unlikely depots suggests the Hereford Shed Running Foreman is a little desperate and made use of visiting spare freight engines. One hopes they get returned from this little venture before their Monday balanced workings. John Goss

Branch track lifting train. It is eight months since branch closure and a contractor's train is working near Ballingham between Ross-on-Wye and Hereford recovering redundant track. The lifting is taking place from the Ross-on-Wye end, and Gloucester's 3F 0-6-0PT No. 3616 and its footplate crew are spending a leisurely day working to the contractor's instructions. JOHN GOSS

Leominster's second engine, the 2F 7400 0-6-0PT, was, meanwhile, working the Kington branch freight trip. In the summer 1960 timetable, this departed from Leominster on Mondays to Saturdays at 8.20am for Kington. Typically, No. 7426 worked the service on 20 May and 4 June 1960, the trip being booked to shunt intermediately at Kingsland and Pembridge. The engine then ran round its train at Kington, passenger and freight services having been withdrawn beyond to New Radnor in 1951, although the initial part of the latter line had remained open to Dolyhir Quarry until June 1958. Having run round its train at Kington, berthing wagons as necessary, the trip headed for Presteign, as railway timetables quaintly spelt it, rather than Presteigne as it was known by the wider community. After shunting and berthing wagons, it returned to Kington, ran around its train once again and performed more shunting as required. No doubt the crew then took a well-earned lunch break before the return trip to Leominster, arriving back at 3.40pm. On Saturdays, a shortened schedule applied and the trip returned at lunchtime.

The branch freight duties were taken over by a 1P 1400 0-4-2T from February 1962, possibly to reduce axle weight on this barely-maintained branch line. The new arrivals on Hereford's allocation were Nos. 1420 and 1447 from Exeter and Croes Newydd. One would, as usual, be out-based at Leominster whilst the other was held spare at Hereford. In July 1963, a third engine, No. 1458, arrived from Oswestry, but was put into store at Hereford initially until February 1964 when No. 1447 left for Gloucester. No. 1458 is remembered for still carrying its 89D Oswestry shed plate throughout its time at Hereford, no doubt confusing visiting railway enthusiasts. Leominster

Shed closed in April 1962, with the branch engine then coming out from Hereford each morning.

By the winter 1963 timetable the trip had been reduced to Tuesdays, Thursdays and Saturdays only, with the Saturday service still returning home earlier at lunchtime. The schedule itself remained very similar with only detailed timing differences. The branch engine was still booked out from Hereford to Leominster on Mondays, Wednesdays and Fridays when the trip did not run, to perform 7.55am to 3pm shunting duties servicing the goods depot, mileage yard and engineers sidings. In 1964, the branch enjoyed an unexpected temporary upturn in traffic to Presteigne, when metal pipes were conveyed for a gas pipeline under construction in the area.

The branch freight service was formally withdrawn from 28 September 1964, with No. 1420 working on the final day, the previous Thursday. This was yet another part of a co-ordinated strategy towards final closure of Hereford Shed, with the former Brecon line freight trip taken off from the same date. A month later the Hereford to Gloucester passenger and freight service was also withdrawn, and Hereford Shed closed.

It appears that in the final year of operations, and contrary to surviving timetable records, Hereford would send out both 1400s on branch trip days, with one spending the day shunting at Leominster whilst the other worked the branch trip. A filmed record on 28 April 1964 clearly shows No. 1420 arriving back with the afternoon trip whilst No. 1458 shunts in the background. Both engines are then shown departing coupled light engine for Hereford. I personally recorded on several late-afternoon Hereford Shed visits, both 1400s standing together on the coaling stage road for disposal and servicing.

Leominster Passenger Auto-Train Service
Leominster Shed - 1 x 1400 0-4-2T
Summer 1960 Timetable Morning Service

Location	Times		Remarks
	Arrive	Depart	
	am	am	
Leominster	-	6.45	Passenger Service
Ludlow	7.04	7.22	Train reverses
Woofferton	7.30	7.35	Train reverses
Tenbury Wells	7.45	7.55	Train reverses
Woofferton	8.05	8.10	Train reverses
Ludlow	8.20	8.22	Train reverses
Woofferton	8.30	8.33	Train reverses
Tenbury Wells	8.42	8.50	Train reverses
Leominster	9.13	-	Light Engine to shed

Afternoon auto duties are about to commence on 29 June 1961 with No1445 heading the 3.50pm Leominster to Ludlow, where it would then form the 4.15pm to Tenbury Wells school service. It would be wonderful to imagine this little train progressing St Trinian's style, with screaming school children hanging out of the windows waving hockey sticks, but I suspect although noisy it was not quite like that. R.G. NELSON/TERRY WALSH COLLECTION

Locomotive storage from Shrewsbury or Cambrian depots was common at Craven Arms, notably in the winter when extra summer engines were surplus to requirements. Croes Newydd's Collett 2P 4-4-0 No. 9014 was the hidden jewel found at the back of Craven Arms Shed in 1959. It had spent alternate summers working, and each winter between 1956 and 1960 stored, until final withdrawal in October 1960. John Goss

Knighton banking duties on the Central Wales line, twelve miles from Craven Arms, had historically been covered from the Knighton Sub-shed, an out-base of Shrewsbury. Shrewsbury's 3MT 2251 0-6-0 No. 2214 is seen performing banking duties here in 1961. By the time Hereford assumed responsibility for Craven Arms in January 1963, Knighton Shed had closed and the banking engine came light engine from Craven Arms daily, now one of the Hereford-allocated 3MT 2251 0-6-0s. Author's collection

Hereford Shed – Rundown and Closure

For many years, the relatively local nature of Hereford's locomotive work, although its footplate crews ventured far and wide, had protected it from the march of dieselisation on main-line passenger and parcels services passing through the area. Main-line freight would however remain almost exclusively steam hauled until diesel incursions began in spring 1964. However, the loss of the Depot's remaining main-line passenger work and departure in late June 1964 of its four remaining 7P Castle 4-6-0s was an ominous development. Their departure did initially mean an extra 5700 0-6-0PT diagrammed for station pilot duties, whilst in practice a 3MT 2251 0-6-0 or 4MT 5101 2-6-2T might be provided for this turn. No. 4623 was noted on station-pilot duties on 11 July and 16 September, No. 4107 on 20 July, No. 4668 on 29 September, No. 2242 on 18 July and 4 October, and No. 2287 on 18 September 1964. However, the ability of Hereford to provide assistance to ailing locomotives on express-passenger services was now a thing of the past.

Locomotive Allocation – September 1964
86C Hereford

2251 3MT 0-6-0		5700 3F 0-6-0PT		Drewry 204hp Shunter	
2242	2287	3683	4623	D2200*	D2235
		3728	4668	D2207	D2238
				D2219	
				*Officially allocated. Did not arrive in practice.	
5101 4MT 2-6-2T		**1600 2F 0-6-0PT**			
4107	4161	1613	1657	**Total Steam: 13**	
4157		1631	1667	**Total Diesel: 5**	

Last day of service on the Hereford to Gloucester branch on Saturday, 31 October 1964. Hereford's 4MT 2-6-2T No. 4107 takes water at Gloucester Central before departure with the 12.15pm to Hereford. No. 4107 had worked the 7.30am Hereford over that morning and would do a second round trip with the 4.30pm Hereford to Gloucester, returning on the penultimate 7.15pm Gloucester to Hereford. JOHN GOSS

Now, the Depot's 4MT 5101 2-6-2Ts and 3MT 2251 0-6-0s were the largest engines on the allocation. By late June 1964, this was down to seventeen engines comprising three 5101 4MT 2-6-2Ts; three 2251 3MT 0-6-0s; five 3F 5700 0-6-0PTs; four 2F 1600 0-6-0PTs and two 1400 1P 0-4-2Ts. The Shed was by now looking considerably quieter with much fewer visiting main-line freight engines as freight trains became progressively dieselised. However, home-based local passenger and freight working levels were still largely being maintained.

Behind the scenes, though, the powers that be were putting into place a series of planned branch passenger and freight service withdrawals, combined with plans to replace the area's yard work with diesel shunting engines. This would happen in a surprisingly short period of time, between August and November 1964. The changes started with five Drewry 204hp diesel shunting engines, Nos. D2200, 2219, 2235, 2238 and 2240, being allocated to Hereford in August 1964. Rather oddly, these were not internal WR transfers, but from the Eastern Region at March, Norwich and Colwich. D2200 never actually arrived in practice, but the other four were only gradually introduced onto shunting duties, with several turns remaining steam worked right up until Depot closure.

The next casualties were the freight trips from Hereford to Eardisley and Leominster to Kington, which were withdrawn and both branch lines closed from 28 September 1964. The Kington withdrawal marked the end for Hereford's diminutive 1P 1400 0-4-2Ts. No. 1458 was transferred to Gloucester in July 1964, leaving No. 1420 to follow after line closure. Both engines joined other Gloucester class members working the Chalford auto service during its final month of operation until withdrawal from the same date as Hereford-Gloucester services from Monday, 2 November 1964.

The Shed entered its final month of operations in October 1964, with an allocation of twelve steam locomotives and the five Drewry 204hp diesel shunting engines. That fifth diesel shunting engine, No. D2200, was still noticeable by its absence and never would arrive at the Depot. The twelve steam locomotive allocation was by no means generous for the remaining workload, bearing in mind variable locomotive condition as closure loomed. The final month's residents comprised two 3MT 2251 0-6-0s with two booked freight diagrams and no spare cover; three 4MT 5101 2-6-2Ts covering the two

intensive Hereford-Gloucester passenger diagrams with one engine spare; three 3F 5700 0-6-0PTs for the Hereford Station pilot and out-based Craven Arms shunting turn leaving one engine spare; and four 2F 1600 0-6-0PTs booked to cover the Pontrilas freight trip and two residual freight shunting turns, leaving again just one engine spare. Two further freight shunting turns were diagrammed to be covered by the Drewry 204hp diesel shunters, a rather gentle introduction to the Depot's workload. No fuelling facilities were available for these at the Shed and when required it was taken at the DMU stabling sidings beside the main line south of the Station.

Typically, and not for the last time, the LMR struggled to keep pace with dieselisation on cross,-boundary services. The two daily Shrewsbury-Hereford pick-up freights remained stubbornly steam hauled. On each of these weekday visits, there had been just four or five of Hereford's twelve remaining allocated engines on Shed, either having recently returned from their daily duties or occasionally standing spare. My very last shed visit was on Friday, 30 October, with Hereford-Gloucester services and all local work to finish the next day, although the formal closure date would be Monday, 2 November 1964. It was around midday and I was greeted by Shrewsbury BR Standard 4MT 2-6-4T No. 80135 on the turntable, having recently come on shed having covered the early-morning Gloucester passenger round trip. This was a likely indication that the Shed Running Foreman had been short of available home-based locomotives that morning. In a final flurry of activity, visitors from other depots on that final Friday, 30 October included Ebbw Junction's 8F 2884 2-8-0 No. 3807, Worcester's 5MT 4-6-0 No. 6819 *Highnam Grange*, Shrewsbury's 5MT 4-6-0

Appendix VI

Hereford Shed – Locomotive Diagrams Summary
Four Weeks Ending: 18 May 1963

Engine Class	Passgr.	Freight	Goods Shunt	Passgr. Shunt	Banking	Pilot	Specials	Total	Engines Allocated
Hall 4-6-0	2					1		3	5
2251 0-6-0		1						1	2
5101 2-6-2T	2							2	3
5700 0-6-0PT			2.5					2.5	4
7400 0-6-0PT								0	1
1600 0-6-0PT		2	1					3	4
1400 0-4-2T		1						1	2
78000 2-6-0		1						1	1
82000 2-6-2T								0	0
Total	**4**	**5**	**3.5**			**1**		**13.5**	**22**
Craven Arms Sub-shed	Passgr.	Freight	Goods Shunt	Passgr. Shunt	Banking	Pilot	Specials	Total	Engines Allocated
2251 0-6-0					1			1	1
5700 0-6-0PT			1					1	1
Total			**1**		**1**			**2**	**2**
Grand Total	**4**	**5**	**4.5**		**1**	**1**		**15.5**	**24**

Engine Class	Workload Summary – 4 w/e 18 May 1963
Hall	1 x Pass. Cardiff-North-West, 1 x Pass. Hereford-Worcester, 1 x Station Pilot
2251	1 x Gloucester Branch Freight, cover for 5101s and 78000 as necessary
5101	2 x Gloucester Branch Pass. Turns (total five round trips). Replaced 82000s.
5700	2.5 x Yard Shunting Turns Hereford (inc. inter-yard trips)
1600	3 x Yard Shunting/Freight Trips (inc. Pontrilas and Rotherwas freight trips)
1400	1 x Leominster – Kington Branch Freight
78000	1 x Eardisley Branch Freight (former Brecon line)
2251	Craven Arms Sub-Shed: 1 x Banking Turn Knighton (Central Wales line)
5700	Craven Arms Sub-Shed: 1 x Freight Shunting Turn Craven Arms/Ludlow

Appendix VII

Hereford Shed – Locomotive Diagrams Summary
Four Weeks Ending: 2 November 1963

Engine Class	Passgr.	Freight	Goods Shunt	Passgr. Shunt	Banking	Pilot	Specials	Total	Engines Allocated
Castle 4-6-0	3							3	3
Hall 4-6-0								0	2
2251 0-6-0		1						1	3
5101 2-6-2T	2							2	3
5700 0-6-0PT			2.5					2.5	4
1600 0-6-0PT		2	1					3	4
1400 0-4-2T		1						1	2
78000 2-6-0		1						1	1
Total	**5**	**5**	**3.5**					**13.5**	**22**
Craven Arms Sub-shed	Passgr.	Freight	Goods Shunt	Passgr. Shunt	Banking	Pilot	Specials	Total	Engines Allocated
5700 0-6-0PT			1					1	1
Grand Total	**5**	**5**	**4.5**					**14.5**	**23**

Engine Class	Workload Summary – 4 w/e 2 November 1963
Castle	1 x Pass. Cardiff-North-West, 1 x Pass. Hereford-Worcester, 1 x Station Pilot
Hall	No work – Castles taken over duties. Engines awaiting transfer away
2251	1 x Gloucester and Lydbrook Branch Freight, cover for 5101s and 78000
5101	2 x Gloucester Branch Pass. Turns (total five round trips)
5700	2.5 x Yard Shunting Turns Hereford (inc. inter-yard trips)
1600	3 x Yard Shunting/Freight Trips (inc. Pontrilas and Rotherwas freight trips)
1400	1 x Leominster – Kington Branch Freight
78000	1 x Eardisley Branch Freight (former Brecon line)
5700	Craven Arms Sub-shed: 1 x Freight Shunting Turn Craven Arms/Ludlow

Appendix VIII

Hereford Shed – Locomotive Diagrams Summary
Four Weeks Ending: 25 January 1964

Engine Class	Passgr.	Freight	Goods Shunt	Passgr. Shunt	Banking	Pilot	Specials	Total	Engines Allocated
Castle 4-6-0	3							3	4
2251 0-6-0		2						2	3
5101 2-6-2T	2							2	3
5700 0-6-0PT			2.5					2.5	4
1600 0-6-0PT		2	1					3	3
1400 0-4-2T		1						1	3
78000 2-6-0								0	0
Total	**5**	**5**	**3.5**					**13.5**	**20**

Craven Arms Sub-shed	Passgr.	Freight	Goods Shunt	Passgr. Shunt	Banking	Pilot	Specials	Total	Engines Allocated
5700 0-6-0PT			1					1	1
Grand Total	**5**	**5**	**4.5**					**14.5**	**21**

Engine Class	Workload Summary – 4 w/e 25 January 1964
Castle	1 x Pass. Cardiff-North-West, 1 x Pass. Hereford-Worcester, 1 x Station Pilot
2251	1 x Gloucester and Lydbrook Branch Freight, 1 x Eardisley Branch Freight
5101	2 x Gloucester Branch Pass. Turns (total five round trips)
5700	2.5 x Yard Shunting Turns Hereford (inc. inter-yard trips)
1600	3 x Yard Shunting/Freight Trips (inc. Pontrilas and Rotherwas freight trips)
1400	1 x Leominster – Kington Branch Freight
78000	Transferred away – 2251 taken over Eardisley Branch Freight
5700	Craven Arms Sub-shed:1 x Freight Shunting Turn Craven Arms/Ludlow

Appendix IX

Hereford Shed – Locomotive Diagrams Summary
Four Weeks Ending: 11 July 1964

Engine Class	Passgr.	Freight	Goods Shunt	Passgr. Shunt	Banking	Pilot	Specials	Total	Engines Allocated
Castle 4-6-0								0	0
2251 0-6-0		2						2	3
5101 2-6-2T	2							2	3
5700 0-6-0PT			2.5			1		3.5	4
1600 0-6-0PT		2	1					3	4
1400 0-4-2T		1						1	2
Total	**2**	**5**	**3.5**			**1**		**11.5**	**16**
Craven Arms Sub-shed	**Passgr.**	**Freight**	**Goods Shunt**	**Passgr. Shunt**	**Banking**	**Pilot**	**Specials**	**Total**	**Engines Allocated**
5700 0-6-0PT			1					1	1
Grand Total	**5**	**5**	**4.5**					**14.5**	**21**

Engine Class	Workload Summary – 4 w/e 11 July 1964
Castle	Transferred Away – Main-line work dieselised, Station Pilot now 5700
2251	1 x Gloucester and Lydbrook Branch Freight, 1 x Eardisley Branch Freight
5101	2 x Gloucester Branch Pass. Turns (total five round trips)
5700	2.5 x Yard Shunting Turns Hereford (inc. inter-yard trips), 1 x Station Pilot
1600	3 x Yard Shunting/Freight Trips (inc. Pontrilas and Rotherwas freight trips)
1400	1 x Leominster – Kington Branch Freight
5700	Craven Arms Sub-shed: 1 x Freight Shunting Turn Craven Arms/Ludlow

Appendix X

Hereford Shed – Locomotive Diagrams Summary
Four Weeks Ending: 3 October 1964

Engine Class	Passgr.	Freight	Goods Shunt	Passgr. Shunt	Banking	Pilot	Specials	Total	Engines Allocated
2251 0-6-0		1	1					2	2
5101 2-6-2T	2							2	3
5700 0-6-0PT						1		1	3
1600 0-6-0PT		1	2					3	4
1400 0-4-2T								0	0
Total	**2**	**2**	**3**			**1**		**8**	**12**

Craven Arms Sub-shed	Passgr.	Freight	Goods Shunt	Passgr. Shunt	Banking	Pilot	Specials	Total	Engines Allocated
5700 0-6-0PT			1					1	1
Steam Grand Total	**2**	**2**	**4**			**1**		**9**	**13**

Engine Class	Workload Summary – 4 w/e 3 October 1964
2251	1 x Gloucs. and Lydbrook Freight, 1 x Goods Shunt, Eardisley Freight withdrawn
5101	2 x Gloucester Branch Pass. Turns (total five round trips)
5700	1 x Station Pilot , Yard Shunting Turns lost to Diesel Shunters
1600	3 x Yard Shunting/Freight Trips (inc. Pontrilas and Rotherwas freight trips)
1400	Transferred Away - Leominster to Kington Branch Freight withdrawn
Class 03	2 x Yard Shunting Hereford (vice 5700s) and Class 03 training
5700	Craven Arms Sub-shed: 1 x Freight Shunting Turn Craven Arms/Ludlow

Appendix XI

Hereford Shed – Locomotive Diagrams Summary
Four Weeks Ending: 31 October 1964
Final Period before Shed Closure

Engine Class	Passgr.	Freight	Goods Shunt	Passgr. Shunt	Banking	Pilot	Specials	Total	Engines Allocated
2251 0-6-0		1	1					2	2
5101 2-6-2T	2							2	3
5700 0-6-0PT						1		1	2
1600 0-6-0PT		1	1					2	4
Total	**2**	**2**	**2**			**1**		**7**	**11**
Craven Arms Sub-shed	**Passgr.**	**Freight**	**Goods Shunt**	**Passgr. Shunt**	**Banking**	**Pilot**	**Specials**	**Total**	**Engines Allocated**
5700 0-6-0PT			1					1	1
Steam Grand Total	**2**	**2**	**3**			**1**		**8**	**12**
Hereford Diesels	**Passgr.**	**Freight**	**Goods Shunt**	**Passgr. Shunt**	**Banking**	**Pilot**	**Specials**	**Total**	**Engines Allocated**
Class 03 204hp Shunter		1	2					3	5

Engine Class	Workload Summary – 4 w/e 31 October 1964
2251	1 x Gloucester and Lydbrook Branch Freight, 1 x Goods Shunt
5101	2 x Gloucester Branch Pass. Turns (total five round trips)
5700	1 x Station Pilot , Yard Shunting Turns lost to Diesel Shunters
1600	2 x Yard Shunting/Freight Trips
1400	Transferred Away - Leominster to Kington Branch Freight withdrawn
Class 03	3 x Yard Shunting/Freight Trip Hereford (vice 5700s and 1600)
5700	Craven Arms Sub-shed: 1 x Freight Shunting Turn Craven Arms/Ludlow

Bibliography

HODGE, John, *The North & West Route – Shrewsbury
& Hereford* , Wild Swan Publications 2008

LONGWORTH, Hugh, *BR Steam Locomotives Complete Allocations
History 1948-1968*, OPC (an input of Ian Allan Publications) 2014

LYONS, E, *An Historical Survey of Great Western Engine
Sheds*, Oxford Publishing Co. 1974

SIXSMITH, Ian, *The Book of the Castle 4-6-0s*, Irwell Press Ltd. 2009

SMITH, William H, *The Hereford, Hay and Brecon Branch*, KRM Publishing 2008

WOOD, Gordon, *Railways of Hereford*, Amadeus Press 2003

Journals and records

BR–WR Engine Record Cards AN7/116-126, National Archives, Kew

BR–WR Engine Diagram Summary by Shed 1963/64
AN7/85 and 86, National Archives, Kew

BR-WR Working Timetables, Various 1958-1964

Railway Locomotives, British Locomotive Society Journal, Monthly 1958-64

Trains Illustrated/Modern Railways, Monthly 1958-1964